Debbie Mumm's
Greenwood Gardens

Dear Friends,

What a wonderful world we live in! All I have to do is look out the window to find ample inspiration for my art and quilt designs. For this book, we traveled just a few miles farther to a farming community called "Davenport." Residents John and Pam Greenwood graciously shared their acres of gardens for inspiration and photography of our garden and outdoor-themed quilts.

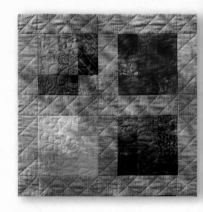

We chose the location first and then had a great time designing quilts around their garden beds and, in some cases, they were kind enough to design the garden beds around our quilts! The end result is this beautiful book—and more than 25 fun projects for you to enjoy as you sew and decorate your home.

I think you'll find many projects to intrigue you, and all were designed to feature fast and easy construction techniques like strip-piecing and Quick Corner Triangles. Choose from fascinating bed quilts like Earth and Water or Marigold Morning; decorate with wall quilts like Fabric Foliage and Autumn Treasures; or accessorize your home and garden with projects like the Sunflower Window or Rooster Banner. You'll have as much fun making these projects as you will showing them off in your home.

So, pour yourself a cup of green tea and relax as you take a look through this new book designed to fill you with inspiration and give you a great assortment of new projects. Now, the hard part will be deciding which project to do first!

All My Best,
Debbie
Mumm

Contents

Marigold Morning

Awaken each morning to the sunny sensation of summer with this beautiful quilt on your bed. Marigolds bloom in a starry formation enclosed in Irish Chain furrows that extend into the border for a charming new look.

Marigold Morning
Bed Quilt

Marigold Morning Bed Quilt Finished Size: 73"x 86½"	FIRST CUT		SECOND CUT	
	Number of Strips or Pieces	Dimensions	Number of Pieces	Dimensions
Fabric A Star Background and Nine-Patch Squares 2¼ yards	3	4½" x 42"	40	4½" x 2½"
	8	2½" x 42"	80	2½" squares
	11	2" x 42"		
	17	1¼" x 42"	20	1¼" x 14"
			20	1¼" x 12½"
Fabric B Cross Hatch Block Background 1⅛ yards	5	5" x 42"	40	5" squares
	Border			
	5	2" x 42"		
Fabric C Star and Nine-Patch Red Squares 3⅞ yards	5	4½" x 42"	40	4½" squares
	3	2½" x 42"		
	9	2" x 42"		
	Border			
	1	9½" x 42"	4	9½" squares
	7	5" x 42"	54	5" squares
	5	3½" x 42"		
	11	2" x 42"	10	2" x 5"
Fabric D Gold Star Center ⅔ yard	2	4½" x 42"	10	4½" squares
	5	2½" x 42"	80	2½" squares
Fabric E Nine-Patch Stripe Squares ⅝ yard	4	2" x 42"		
	Border			
	6	2" x 42"		
Binding ¾ yard	9	2¾" x 42"		
Backing - 5¼ yards Batting - 80" x 94"				

Star Blocks and Cross Hatch Blocks alternate throughout this quilt. The pieced border continues the flow of the blocks and adds rhythm and sophistication to the quilt.

Fabric Requirements and Cutting Instructions

Read all instructions before beginning and use ¼"-wide seam allowances throughout. Read Cutting Strips and Pieces on page 92 prior to cutting fabrics.

Getting Started

Refer to Accurate Seam Allowance on page 92. Whenever possible, use the Assembly Line Method on page 92. Press seams in direction of arrows. Blocks measure 14" square.

Making the Star Block

1. Sew one 2½" x 42" Fabric A strip and one 2½" x 42" Fabric C strip together as shown to make a strip set. Press. Make three. Cut forty 2½"-wide segments from strip sets.

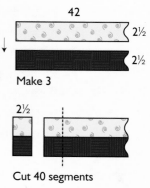

Make 3

Cut 40 segments

2. Sew one 4½" x 2½" Fabric A piece and one segment from step 1 together as shown. Press. Make forty.

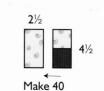

Make 40

3. Refer to Quick Corner Triangles on page 92. Making quick corner triangle units, sew two 2½" Fabric A squares and two 2½" Fabric D squares to one 4½" Fabric C square as shown. Press. Make forty.

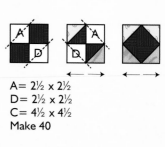

A = 2½ x 2½
D = 2½ x 2½
C = 4½ x 4½
Make 40

4. Sew one unit from step 3 between two units from step 2 as shown. Press. Make twenty.

Make 20

5. Sew one 4½" Fabric D square between two units from step 3 as shown. Press. Make ten.

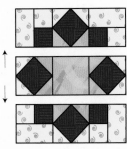

4½

4½

Make 10

6. Sew one unit from step 5 between two units from step 4 as shown. Press. Make ten.

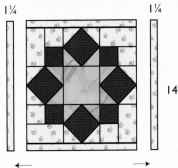

Make 10

7. Sew unit from step 6 between two 1¼" x 12½" Fabric A pieces. Press. Sew this unit between two 1¼" x 14" Fabric A pieces as shown. Press. Make ten. Block measures 14" square.

1¼   1¼

14

Make 10
Star Block measures 14" square

Making the
Cross Hatch Block

1. Sew one 2" x 42" Fabric E strip, one 2" x 42" Fabric A strip, and one 2" x 42" Fabric C strip together as shown to make a strip set. Press. Make four. Cut eighty 2"-wide segments from strip sets.

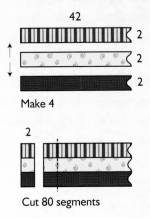

42

2

2

2

Make 4

2

Cut 80 segments

Marigold Morning Bed Quilt
Finished Size: 73" x 86½"

2. Sew one 2" x 42" Fabric A strip between two 2" x 42" Fabric C strips as shown to make a strip set. Press. Cut twenty 2"-wide segments from strip set.

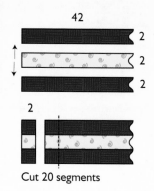

42

2
2
2

2

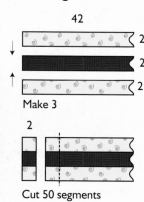

Cut 20 segments

3. Sew one 2" x 42" Fabric C strip between two 2" x 42" Fabric A strips as shown to make a strip set. Press. Make three. Cut fifty 2"-wide segments from strip set.

42

2
2
2

Make 3

2

Cut 50 segments

4. Sew one segment from step 3 between two segments from step 1 as shown. Press. Make twenty.

Make 20

5. Sew one segment from step 3 between two segments from step 1 as shown. Press. Make twenty.

Make 20

6. Sew one segment from step 3 between two segments from step 2 as shown. Press. Make ten.

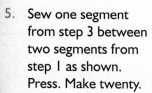
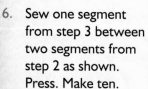

Make 10

7. Sew one 5" Fabric B square between one unit from step 4 and one unit from step 5 as shown. Press. Make twenty.

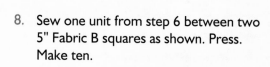

5

5

Make 20

8. Sew one unit from step 6 between two 5" Fabric B squares as shown. Press. Make ten.

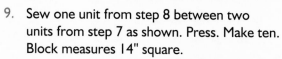

5   5

5

Make 10

9. Sew one unit from step 8 between two units from step 7 as shown. Press. Make ten. Block measures 14" square.

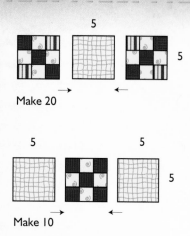

Make 10
Block measures 14" square

Assembly

1. Sew Star Blocks and Cross Hatch Blocks together in pairs as shown. Press. Make ten. Referring to photo on page 4 and layout on page 7, arrange and sew two units together to make a row. Make five rows. Press seams in opposite directions from row to row.

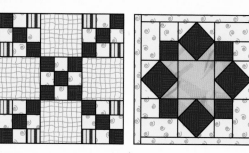

Make 10

2. Referring to photo on page 4 and layout on page 7 sew rows together. Press.

Making Border Block One

1. Sew one 3½" x 42" Fabric C strip and one 2" x 42" Fabric B strip together as shown to make a strip set. Press. Make three. Cut forty-eight 2" wide segments from strip sets.

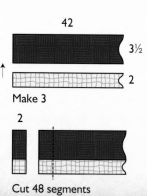

42

3½
2

Make 3

2

Cut 48 segments

2. Sew one 2" x 42" Fabric B strip between two 2" x 42" Fabric C strips as shown to make a strip set. Press. Make two. Cut twenty-four 2"-wide segments from strip sets as shown.

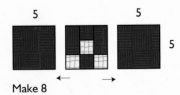

Make 2

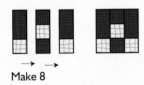

Cut 24 segments

3. Sew one unit from step 2 between two units from step 1 as shown. Press. Make sixteen.

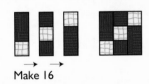

Make 16

4. Sew one unit from step 2 between two units from step 1 as shown. Press. Make eight.

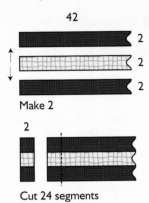

Make 8

5. Sew one unit from step 4 between two 5" Fabric C squares as shown. Press. Make eight.

Make 8

6. Sew one 5" Fabric C square between two units from step 3 as shown. Press. Make eight.

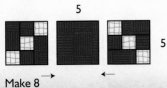

Make 8

7. Sew units from steps 5 and 6 together in pairs as shown. Press half in one direction and half in the opposite direction. Make eight. Border Block One measures 14" x 9½".

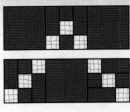

Make 8
Border Block One measures 14 x 9½

8. Referring to photo on page 4 and layout on page 7, sew together four of Border Block One to make a border row. Press seams opposite from top row of quilt top. Make two. Sew rows to top and bottom of quilt. Press seams toward border.

Making Border Block Two

1. Sew one 3½" x 42" Fabric C strip and one 2" x 42" Fabric E strip together as shown to make a strip set. Press. Make two. Cut forty 2"-wide segments from strip sets.

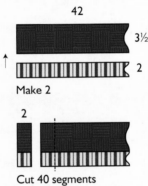

Make 2

Cut 40 segments

2. Sew one 2" x 42" Fabric E strip between two 2" x 42" Fabric C strips as shown to make a strip set. Press. Make two. Cut thirty 2"-wide segments from strip set.

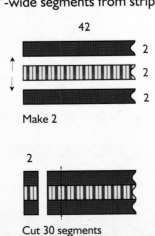

Make 2

Cut 30 segments

3. Sew one 2" x 42" Fabric C strip between two 2" x 42" Fabric E strips as shown to make a strip set. Press. Cut ten 2"-wide segments from strip set.

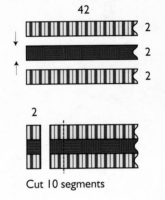

Cut 10 segments

4. Sew one segment from step 2 between one 2" x 5" Fabric C piece and one segment from step 3 as shown. Press. Make ten and label Unit 1.

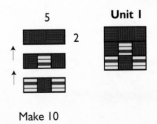

Make 10

5. Sew one unit from step 2 between two units from step 1 as shown to make Unit 2. Press. Make ten and label Unit 2. Sew one unit from step 2 between two units from step 1 as shown to make Unit 3. Press. Make ten and label Unit 3.

Unit 2

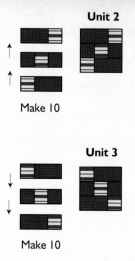

Make 10

Unit 3

Make 10

Layering and Finishing

1. Cut backing crosswise into two equal pieces. Sew pieces together to make one 80" x 94"(approximate) backing piece. Press.

2. Arrange and baste backing, batting, and top together referring to Layering the Quilt on page 94.

3. Machine or hand quilt as desired.

4. Sew 2¾"-wide binding strips together end-to-end to make one continuous 2¾"-wide binding strip. Refer to Binding the Quilt on page 94 and bind quilt to finish.

6. Sew one Unit 1 between two 5" Fabric C squares as shown. Press. Make ten.

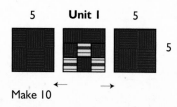

5   **Unit 1**   5

5

Make 10

7. Sew one 5" Fabric C square between one Unit 2 and one Unit 3 as shown. Press. Make ten.

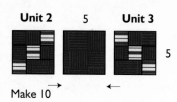

Unit 2   5   **Unit 3**

5

Make 10

8. Sew units from steps 6 and 7 together as shown. Press half in one direction and half in the opposite direction. Make ten. Border Block Two measures 14" x 9½".

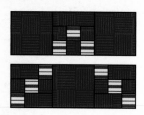

Make 10
Border Block Two measures 14 x 9½

9. Referring to photo on page 4 and layout on page 7, sew five of Border Block Two together to make a row. Press seams opposite from quilt sides. Make two.

10. Sew one border unit from step 9 between two 9½" Fabric C squares. Press seams toward Fabric C. Make two and sew to sides of quilt. Press.

Marigold Morning

Flower Bucket

Show off the beautiful blooms of summer in this French bucket–the perfect backdrop for colorful bouquets. Embossed designs are achieved with dimensional paint and stencils. We used a quilting stencil for the top design, so check out your stash before heading to the craft store! Decorative gems provide additional sparkle and dimension to this beautiful vase.

Painting the Bucket

Refer to General Painting Directions on page 95. Thoroughly wash the tin bucket with vinegar, rinse wih water, and allow to dry. The vinegar removes oils from the bucket that are left from the manufacturing process.

1. When thoroughly dry, spray bucket inside and out with metal primer. Allow to dry.

2. Tape stencil in place at top of bucket. Using a palette knife, apply dimensional paint to the stencil as shown.

3. While paint is wet, carefully remove stencil by lifting straight up as shown. Wash stencil with water and dry with paper towel. Allow paint to dry.

4. Repeat process on the other side of the bucket and on the bottom area. Allow dimensional paint to dry thoroughly between applications.

5. Paint outside of bucket and at least 2-3" inside with Tompte Red paint. Two coats may be needed for good coverage. Allow to dry.

6. Spray bucket with matte varnish.

7. Following directions on the bottle, apply Antiquing Medium to bucket, wiping off Medium until the overall color desired is achieved. Apply a second coat of Antiquing Medium to top and bottom stencil area, wiping medium off the raised areas and allowing it to gather in depressions so that stenciling stands out.

8. When thoroughly dry, spray bucket with matte varnish.

9. Glue decorative gems to bucket as desired.

Supply List

Tin French Bucket

Household Vinegar

Spray Metal Primer

Two Stencils (We used a quilting stencil for the curvy design at the top of the bucket and a geometric stencil for bottom)

Delta Texture Magic™ Dimensional Paint™ 4 Fl. Oz. Tube, any color

Palette Knife

Scotch® Magic™ Tape

Assorted Paintbrushes

Delta Ceramcoat® Acrylic Paint – Tompte Red

Folk Art® Antiquing Medium by Plaid® - Woodn' Bucket Brown

Spray Matte Varnish

Red Decorative Gems

E 6000 Glue

Fabric Foliage

Dappled light dances through the trees highlighting perfect leaves on this fabric tribute to late summer foliage. Easy strip-piecing creates the dappled background and variegated leaves on this beautiful three color quilt.

Fabric Foliage
Wall Quilt

Fabric Foliage Wall Quilt Finished Size: 40½" x 40½"	FIRST CUT	
	Number of Strips or Pieces	Dimensions
Fabric A Background ⅜ yard each of five fabrics	2	11" squares (cut in half diagonally) cut from two different fabrics
	4	10" squares cut from four different fabrics
Fabric B Strip-Pieced Background ⅛ yard each of eleven fabrics	4	1¾" x 42" cut from two different fabrics
	8	1½" x 42" cut from four different fabrics
	4	1¼" x 42" cut from two different fabrics
	6	1" x 42" cut from three different fabrics
Fabric C Strip-Pieced Leaves ⅙ yard each of seven fabrics	8*	1¾" x 21"
	8*	1½" x 21"
	8*	1¼" x 21"
	8*	1" x 21"
		*Cut from assorted green fabrics
Fabric D Whole Leaf Appliqués ¼ yard each of three fabrics		

Fabric Requirements and Cutting Instructions

Read all instructions before beginning and use ¼"-wide seam allowances throughout. Read Cutting Strips and Pieces on page 92 prior to cutting fabrics.

Fabric Foliage Wall Quilt Continued	FIRST CUT	
	Number of Strips or Pieces	Dimensions
BORDERS		
First Border ¼ yard	4	1½" x 42"
Outside Border ⅝ yard	4	5" x 42"
Binding ⅜ yard	4	2¾" x 42"

Backing - 2½ yards
Batting - 45" x 45"
Stem Appliqués - Assorted Scraps
Lightweight Fusible Web - 1¼ yards

The warm, serene colors of late summer are combined to make blocks and leaves for this simple quilt. Some of the leaves and blocks are made with a variety of strip sets while others use solid fabrics for a beautiful mix of colors and techniques.

Getting Started

Refer to Accurate Seam Allowance on page 92. Whenever possible, use the Assembly Line Method on page 92. Press seams in direction of arrows. Blocks measure 10" square unfinished.

Making the Blocks

1. Arrange and sew together four 1½" x 42", two 1¾" x 42", three 1" x 42", and two 1¼" x 42" Fabric B strips as shown to make a 10½" x 42" strip set. Press. Make two.

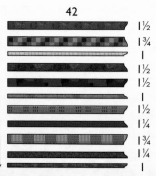

42

1½
1¾
1
1½
1½
1
1½
1¼
1¾
1¼
1

Make 2

2. Cut an 11" square from template material. Cut square in half diagonally to make two equal triangles as shown.

3. Using triangle templates, trace and cut two triangles from strip set unit from step 1 as shown. Cut three 10" squares from strip sets.

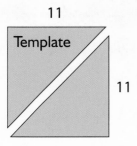

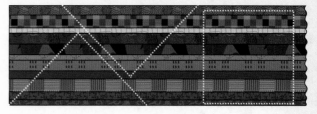

Cut two triangles
Cut three 10" squares

Fabric Foliage Wall Quilt
Finished Size: 40½" x 40½"

4. Sew one strip-pieced triangle from step 3 and one Fabric A triangle together as shown. Press. Square to 10". Make two, one of each combination.

Make 2
(1 of each combination)

5. Referring to photo on page 12 and layout on page 15 arrange and sew four 10" Fabric A squares, three blocks from step 3, and two blocks from step 4 to make three rows of three blocks each. Press seams in opposite directions from row to row.

6. Sew rows together. Press.

Adding the Appliqués

Refer to appliqué instructions on page 93. Our instructions are for Quick-Fuse Appliqué. If you prefer hand appliqué, add ¼"-wide seam allowances to patterns.

1. Arrange and sew assorted 21"-long Fabric C strips to make a strip set. Press. Each strip set should contain a different combination of fabric widths, but must measure at least 7" x 21". Make four.

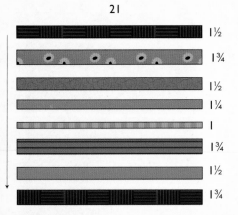

21

1½
1¾
1½
1¼
1
1¾
1½
1¾

Make 4
Varying the widths from set to set in assorted combinations

2. Refer to Quick-Fuse Appliqué on page 93. Use Fabric Foliage patterns on page 17 to trace nine stems, four leaves, and ten half leaves (five right and five left) on paper side of fusible web.

3. Referring to photo on page 12 and layout on page 15 use strip sets from step 1 to prepare ten half leaves (five right and five left) as shown. Use Fabric D to prepare four whole leaves and nine stems.

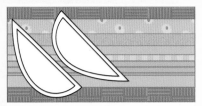

Make 10
(5 of each variation)

4. Referring to photo on page 12 and layout on page 15 position and fuse leaves, half leaves, and stems to quilt top. Finish appliqué edges with machine satin stitch or other decorative stitching as desired.

Adding the Borders

1. Referring to Adding the Borders on page 94, measure quilt through center from side to side. Cut two 1½"-wide First Border strips to this measurement. Sew to top and bottom of quilt. Press seams toward border.

2. Measure quilt through center from top to bottom including borders just added. Cut two 1½"-wide First Border strips to this measurement. Sew to sides of quilt. Press.

3. Refer to steps 1 and 2 to measure, trim, and sew 5"-wide Outside Border strips to top, bottom, and sides of quilt. Press.

Layering and Finishing

1. Cut backing crosswise into two equal pieces. Sew pieces together to make one 45" x 80"(approximate) backing piece. Press and trim to 45" square.

2. Arrange and baste backing, batting, and top together referring to Layering the Quilt on page 94.

3. Machine or hand quilt as desired.

4. Sew 2¾"-wide binding strips end-to-end to make one continuous 2¾"-wide binding strip. Refer to Binding the Quilt on page 94 and bind quilt to finish.

Fabric Foliage

Leaf Wall Art

The bold graphic design of our leaf is softened with glaze and a resist technique to create an art piece for the wall. This technique is so simple and quick to create, you'll want to make a series of art pieces for your home.

We chose to trim the background and mount our leaf on fabric inside a shadow box, but you can also finish your art piece by framing it or decoupaging it to a painted board or canvas.

Supply List

Fabric Scraps for Leaf and Stem

Heavyweight Fusible Web

Tan Heavy Cloth - 10" Square (or larger depending on finishing technique)

Elmer's Glue

Decoupage Medium

Burnt Umber Glaze*

Paintbrush and Rag

Optional: 13½" square shadow box, matboard to fit inside and fabric to cover matboard.

*Mix a few drops of burnt umber acrylic paint with a water-based clear glaze.

1. Refer to Quick Fuse Appliqué on page 93. Prepare and fuse leaf and stem onto heavy cloth.

2. Cover leaf appliqué with decoupage medium and allow to dry. This puts a finish on the leaf so you can control the placement and amount of glaze.

3. Refer to photo and use Elmer's Glue to draw wavy lines on leaf to represent veins. Draw swirls, squiggles, wavy lines on the canvas with the glue. Have fun, you can't do this wrong! Allow glue to dry. The glue becomes a resist, so glaze color will not penetrate as deeply where the glue stops absorption into the fabric.

4. Refer to photo and apply burnt umber glaze to leaf and backing. Allow glaze to collect around the leaf stem, veins, and outside edge and wipe for a lighter appearance on other parts of the leaf. Glaze will color the background cloth allowing squiggles to show. Add more glaze if a deeper color is desired. Allow to dry.

5. To mount in shadow box, roughly trim edges of cloth so it is approximately 8½" square. Cut a piece of matboard to fit inside shadow box and cover with green fabric. Use fabric glue or double-stick tape to affix leaf unit to background.

STEM

Fabric Foliage Wall Quilt
Applique Pattern

Strawberry Fields

Sweet, ripe strawberries top this shortcake of projects adding color and flavor to a fun collection of home decor accessories. Beads and embroidery, bouclé fabrics, and circular appliques bring texture and charming detail to our strawberry collection.

Strawberry Fields
Table Runner

Strawberry Fields Table Runner Finished Size: 36"x 15"	FIRST CUT		SECOND CUT	
	Number of Strips or Pieces	Dimensions	Number of Pieces	Dimensions
Fabric A Center ⅝ yard	1	18½" x 14½"		
Fabric B Accent Strip ⅛ yard	2	1" x 42"	4	1" x 14½"
Fabric C Appliqué Background ⅙ yard	1	3½" x 42"	2	3½" x 14½"
Fabric D Outside Border ¼ yard	1	5½" x 42"	2	5½" x 14½"
Binding ¼ yard	2	2¾" x 42"		

Backing - ⅝ yard
Batting - 40" x 19"
Strawberry Appliqués - ⅛ yard bouclé
Stem Appliqués - Green wool scraps
Lightweight Fusible Web - ⅙ yard

Plump strawberries grow in profusion on this delectable table runner. Luscious stripes and paisley add to the ambiance, but this easy table runner will be the centerpiece of your kitchen in any fabric combination.

Strawberry Fields Table Runner
Finished Size: 36" x 15"

Fabric Requirements and Cutting Instructions

Read all instructions before beginning and use ¼"-wide seam allowances throughout. Read Cutting Strips and Pieces on page 92 prior to cutting fabrics.

Getting Started

Bouclé and wool appliqués decorate this fast and easy table runner. For an unusual treatment we added binding to the long sides only. It is so quick to make, you may want to make two. For directional fabrics, such as our stripe, note direction when cutting the center.

Refer to Accurate Seam Allowance on page 92. Whenever possible, use the Assembly Line Method on page 92. Press seams in direction of arrows.

Making the Quilt Top

Sew together two 5½" x 14½" Fabric D pieces, four 1" x 14½" Fabric B pieces, two 3½" x 14½" Fabric C pieces, and 18½" x 14½" Fabric A piece as shown. Press.

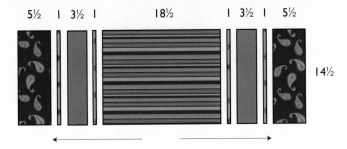

Adding the Appliqués

Refer to appliqué instructions on page 93. Our instructions are for Quick-Fuse Appliqué.

1. Use Strawberry Pattern to trace eight strawberries and eight stems on paper side of fusible web. Use bouclé scraps to prepare strawberries and wool scraps to prepare stems for fusing.

2. Referring to photo and layout, position and fuse appliqués to quilt. Finish appliqué edges with machine satin stitch or other decorative stitching as desired.

Layering and Finishing

1. Cut backing into 40" x 19" piece.

2. Center quilt top on backing, right sides together and place on batting. Using a ¼" seam allowance, stitch short sides of table runner. Trim batting close to stitching, turn right side out, and press seams.

3. Baste quilt (see Layering the Quilt, step 3, on page 94) and machine or hand quilt as desired.

4. Referring to Binding the Quilt on page 94, steps 1 and 2, measure quilt through center from end to end. Cut two binding strips to that measurement plus two inches. Arrange binding strips on top and bottom of quilt extending 1" beyond both sides of quilt. Stitch binding in place. Trim backing and batting ½" beyond seam.

5. Press binding away from quilt top. Fold extensions in toward center, and then fold binding to back. Press and pin in position. Hand-stitch binding in place using a blind stitch (page 95).

Strawberry
Appliqué Pattern
Make 8

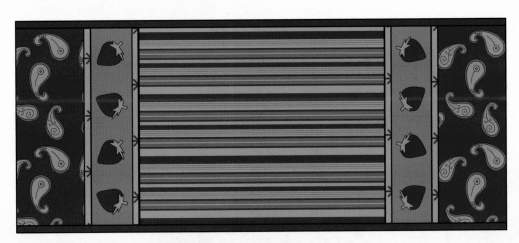

Strawberry Fields Table Runner
Finished Size: 36" x 15"

Strawberry Fields Wallhanging
Finished Size: 15" x 18¾"

Materials Needed

Fabric A (Center)—½ yard bouclé
   One 15" square

Fabric B (Accent Strips)—⅛ yard
   Two 1½" x 15" pieces

Fabric C (Top & Bottom Border)—⅛ yard bouclé
   One 3½" x 15" piece
   One 2¼" x 15" piece

Fabric D (Side Borders)—⅛ yard
   Two 1½" x 19¾" pieces

Lightweight Fusible Interfacing - ¾ yard (optional)

Backing—½ yard

Batting—19" x 23" piece

Circle Appliqués—¼ yard bouclé

Strawberry & Stem Appliqués—Cotton and wool scraps

Lightweight Fusible Web—½ yard

Heavyweight Fusible Web—⅛ yard

Red Embroidery Floss

Assorted Red, Green & Clear Beads

Fabric Glue

Crochet Thread, or Heavy-duty Thread

Bouclé is a creative choice to use in quilting and decorating projects because of the unique texture and loose weave. See tip box on page 23 for bouclé sewing tips.

Making the Wallhanging

1. Use ½"-wide seam allowances throughout. Sew 15" Fabric A square between two 1½" x 15" Fabric B pieces, 2¼" x 15" Fabric C piece, and 3½" x 15" Fabric C piece as shown. Press.

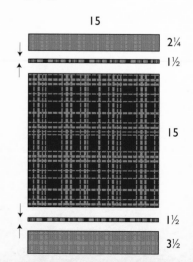

2. Refer to appliqué instructions on page 93. Our instructions are for Quick-Fuse Appliqué. If you prefer hand appliqué, add ¼"-wide seam allowances to patterns. Use pattern on page 25 to trace two Circles, one of each size, on lightweight fusible web. Use bouclé to prepare circles for fusing. Referring to photo, position and fuse circles to wallhanging. (Note: Circle appliqués extend past quilt edges, so use an appliqué pressing sheet to protect ironing surface when pressing.) Trim circles even with quilt top. Finish circle appliqué edges with machine satin stitch or other decorative stitching as desired.

3. Refer to Embroidery Stitch Guide on page 95, photo, and layout. Use six strands of embroidery floss and a running stitch to stitch 4½" and 5½" circles on small circle appliqué and 5¼" and 6¾" circles on large circle appliqué.

4. Referring to appliqué instructions on page 93, use pattern on page 24 to trace three Strawberries, and three Stem appliqués on paper side of heavyweight fusible web. Use cotton for strawberries and wool for stems to prepare appliqués for fusing. Referring to photo and layout, position and fuse appliqués to quilt.

5. Sew appliquéd unit between two 1½" x 19¾" Fabric D pieces as shown. Press.

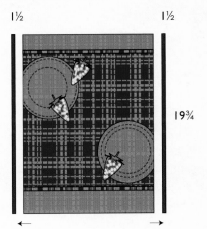

1½   1½

19¾

TIP   SEWING WITH BOUCLÉ

For best results, when sewing larger pieces of bouclé together for a pillow or wallhanging, use fusible lightweight interfacing to provide stability to each piece. Using a boucé piece larger than needed for the project, lay out bouclé on ironing board, keeping pattern and grain of bouclé as square as possible. Following manufacturer's directions, press interfacing to bouclé piece being careful to keep it square. Cut interfacing-backed bouclé to the size needed. Prepare each piece this way to prevent stretching and raveling. Due to the looser weave of bouclé, we recommend using ½" seam allowance when possible

Layering and Finishing

1. Cut backing into 19" x 23" piece.

2. Place wallhanging top and backing right sides together and place wrong side of backing next to batting piece. Using a ½"-wide seam allowance, stitch around edges leaving a 4" opening for turning. Trim batting close to stitching and backing even with top edges. Clip corners, turn right side out, and press. Hand-stitch opening closed.

3. Machine or hand quilt as desired.

4. Referring to photo, glue or sew twenty-five assorted green beads to wallhanging center. Glue assorted red and clear beads to strawberries. Using crochet thread or heavy-duty thread, sew assorted red and green beads to bottom of wallhanging.

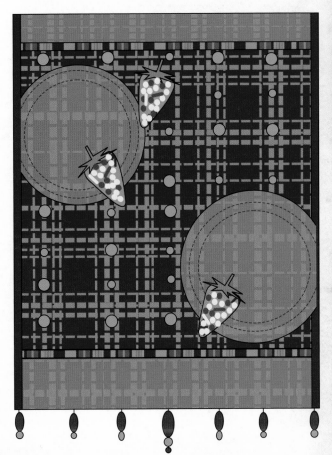

Strawberry Fields Wallhanging
Finished Size: 15" x 18¾"

Lush berries, beads, and embroidery make these pillows perfect decorating accessories.

Strawberry Fields Square Pillow

Materials Needed

Fabric A (Pillow Center)—¼ yard wool
> One 6½" square

Fabric B (Pillow Borders)—⅓ yard wool felt
> Two 4½" x 14½" pieces
> Two 4½" x 6½" pieces

Backing—⅓ yard cotton
> Two 10" x 14½" pieces

Pillow Form Fabric—½ yard
> Two 14½" squares

Polyester Fiberfill

Strawberry & Stem Appliqués—Bouclé
> and felt scraps

Lightweight Fusible Web—⅛ yard

Eight Red Beads

Red & Green Embroidery Floss

Yellow Embroidery Thread

Fabric Requirements and Cutting Instructions

Read all instructions before beginning and use ¼"-wide seam allowances throughout. Read Cutting Strips and Pieces on page 92 prior to cutting fabrics.

Making the Pillow

1. Sew 6½" Fabric A square between two 4½" x 6½" Fabric B pieces as shown.

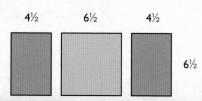

4½   6½   4½

6½

2. Sew unit from step 1 between two 4½" x 14½" Fabric B pieces as shown. Press.

14½

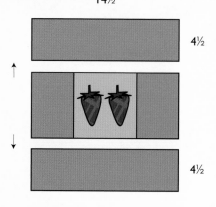

4½

4½

Strawberry and Stem Appliqué Patterns

3. Refer to appliqué instructions on page 93. Our instructions are for Quick-Fuse Appliqué. Use Strawberry pattern to trace two Strawberries and two Stem appliqués on paper side of fusible web. Use bouclé for strawberries and felt for stems to prepare appliqués for fusing.

4. Referring to photo and layout, position and fuse appliqués to pillow. Finish strawberry appliqué edges with machine satin stitch or other decorative stitching as desired. Use six strands of green embroidery floss to tack stems to pillow.

5. Refer to Embroidery Stitch Guide on page 95, photo, and layout. Use six strands of red embroidery floss and a running stitch to stitch a square ½" away from pillow center.

6. Referring to photo and layout, sew decorative stitches parallel to running stitches. We used a Bernina® artista 730, stitch number 115, and yellow thread. Use red embroidery floss to sew beads at each end of decorative stitching.

7. Refer to Finishing Pillows, page 95, steps 2-4, and use two 10" x 14½" backing pieces to finish pillow.

8. Refer to Pillow Forms on page 95 and use two 14½" pillow form squares and fiberfill to make one 14" pillow form.

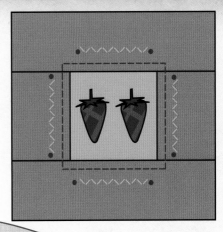

Strawberry Fields Square Pillow
Finished Size: 14" x 14"

Strawberry Fields Circles Pillow

Materials Needed

Pillow Top - ½ yard felt or felted wool
        One 14½" square
Backing - ⅓ yard cotton
        Two 10" x 14½" pieces
Pillow Form Fabric - ½ yard
        Two 14½" squares
Polyester Fiberfill
Circle Appliqués - ¼ yard wool felt
Strawberry & Stem Appliqués - Bouclé and wool scraps
Lightweight Fusible Web - ½ yard
40-50 Assorted Yellow Beads
Red Embroidery Floss

Making the Pillow

1. Refer to appliqué instructions on page 93. Our instructions are for Quick-Fuse Appliqué. Trace two Circles, one of each size, three Strawberries, and three Stem appliqués on paper side of fusible web. Use felt for circles, bouclé for strawberries, and wool for stems to prepare appliqués for fusing.

2. Referring to photo, position and fuse appliqués to 14½" Pillow Top. Note: Circle appliqués extend past pillow edges, so use an appliqué pressing sheet to protect ironing surface. Finish strawberry appliqué edges with machine satin stitch or other decorative stitching as desired. Tack stems in place. Circle edges are not finished. Trim circles even with pillow edges.

3. Refer to Embroidery Stitch Guide on page 95, photo and layout. Use six strands of red embroidery floss and a running stitch to stitch 6¾" and 5½" circles on large circle appliqué and 6" and 4½" circles on small circle appliqué.

4. Refer to Finishing Pillows, page 95, steps 2-4, and use two 10" x 14½" backing pieces to finish pillow.

5. Referring to photo, hand sew beads to edges of circles.

6. Refer to Pillow Forms on page 95 and use two 14½" pillow form squares and fiberfill to make one 14" pillow form.

Strawberry Fields Circles Pillow
Finished Size: 14" x 14"

Circle Patterns

Earth & Water

A soft play of dark and light blocks mimics stones in a flowing brook on this beautiful and unusual bed quilt. All the complexity of this quilt is in the color placement; the blocks are easy to construct. Accent the quilt with a relaxing fountain.

Earth and Water

Queen Bed Quilt

Light, medium, and dark tones symbolize earth, sky, and water on this scrappy quilt. Triangular shapes flow toward the edges of the quilt as the colors change from light to dark.

Earth and Water Queen Bed Quilt Finished Size: 86½"x 106½"	FIRST CUT		SECOND CUT	
	Number of Strips or Pieces	Dimensions	Number of Pieces	Dimensions
Fabric A Dark Tones ⅜ yard each of nine fabrics *Cut for each fabric	1* 1*	6½" x 42" 4½" x 42"	3* 4 * 3*	6½" squares 4½" squares 3½" squares
Fabric B Medium Tones ½ yard each of nine fabrics *Cut for each fabric	1* 1* 1*	6½" x 42" 4½" x 42" 3½" x 42"	3* 7* 1* 3*	6½" squares 4½" squares 4½" x 3½" 3½" squares
Fabric C Light Tones 1⅛ yard each of nine fabrics *Cut for each fabric	5* 4*	4½" x 42" 3½" x 12½"	4* 2* 5* 21* 7* 6* 6*	4½" x 12½" 4½" x 8½" 4½ " squares 4½" x 3½" 3½" x 12½" 3½" x 6½" 3½ " squares
Fabric D Accent Strip ½ yard	10	1¼" x 42"	4	1¼" x 12½"
Binding ⅞ yard	10	2¾" x 42"		
Backing - 8 yards Batting - 95" x 115"				

Fabric Requirements and Cutting Instructions

Read all instructions before beginning and use ¼"-wide seam allowances throughout. Read Cutting Strips and Pieces on page 92 prior to cutting fabrics.

Getting Started

Twelve large blocks (12½" square unfinished) form the basis of the quilt and are enhanced with smaller blocks (8½" square unfinished). The dark-toned blocks form their own design within the quilt to add depth and dimension. Take time to label all blocks and units to simplify assembly.

Refer to Accurate Seam Allowance on page 92. Whenever possible, use the Assembly Line Method on page 92. Press seams in direction of arrows.

Making the Large Block

1. Sew one 3½" Fabric B square to one 3½" Fabric C square as shown. Press. Make twenty-four and label Unit 1. Sew one 3½" Fabric A square to one 3½" Fabric C square as shown. Press. Make twenty-four and label Unit 2.

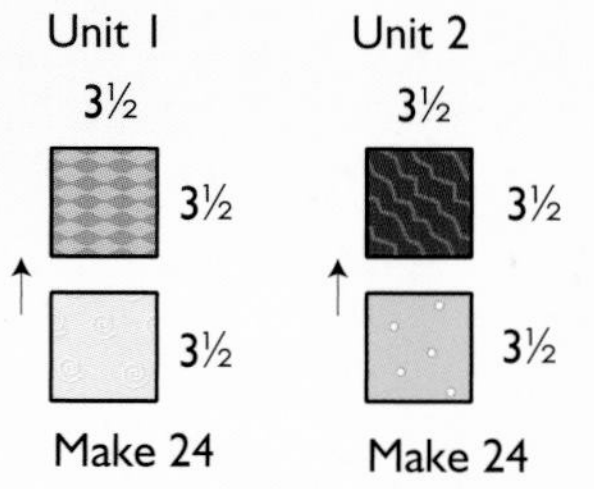

Unit 1
3½
3½
3½
Make 24
Unit 2
3½
3½
3½
Make 24

2. Sew one unit, from step 1, to one 3½" x 6½" Fabric C piece as shown. Press. Make forty-eight, twenty-four of Unit 1 and twenty-four of Unit 2.

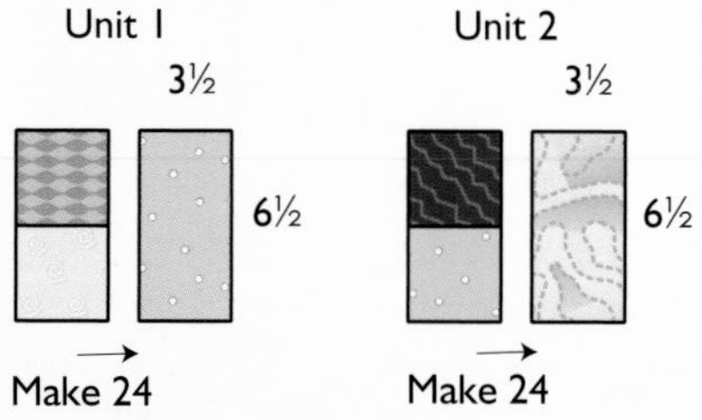

Unit 1
3½
6½
Make 24
Unit 2
3½
6½
Make 24

3. Refer to Quick Corner Triangles on page 92. Making a quick corner triangle unit, sew one Unit 1, from step 2, to one 6½" Fabric B square as shown noting position of seams. Press. Make twenty-four and label Unit 1. Making a quick corner triangle unit, sew one Unit 2, from step 2, to one 6½" Fabric A square as shown noting position of seams. Press. Make twenty-four and label Unit 2.

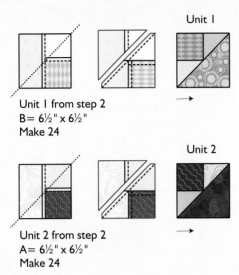

Unit 1

Unit 1 from step 2
B= 6½" x 6½"
Make 24

Unit 2

Unit 2 from step 2
A= 6½" x 6½"
Make 24

4. Sew together two of Unit 1, from step 3, as shown. Press. Make twelve. Sew these units together in pairs as shown. Press. Make six and label Block 1. Block 1 measures 12½" square.

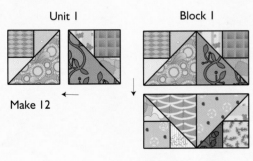

Unit 1   Block 1

Make 12

Make 6
Block 1 measures 12½" square

5. Sew together two of Unit 2, from step 3, as shown. Press. Make twelve. Sew these units together in pairs as shown. Press. Make six and label Block 2. Block 2 measures 12½" square.

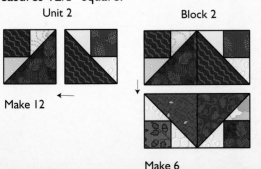

Unit 2   Block 2

Make 12

Make 6
Block 2 measures 12½" square

6. Making a quick corner triangle unit, sew one 4½" Fabric C square and one 4½" Fabric B square together as shown. Press. Make thirty. Label two Unit 3A and set aside. Sew remaining units together in pairs as shown. Press. Make fourteen. Label eight Unit 3B and set aside. Sew two remaining units together as shown to make Block 3. Press. Make three and label Block 3. Block 3 measures 8½" square.

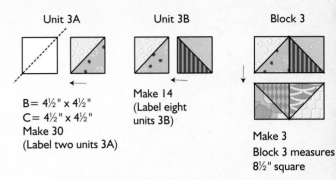

Unit 3A   Unit 3B   Block 3

B= 4½" x 4½"
C= 4½" x 4½"   Make 14
Make 30   (Label eight
(Label two units 3A)   units 3B)

Make 3
Block 3 measures
8½" square

7. Making a quick corner triangle unit, sew one 4½" Fabric A square and one 4½" Fabric C square together as shown. Press. Make fourteen. Label two Unit 4A and set aside. Sew remaining units together in pairs as shown. Press. Make six. Label two Unit 4B and set aside. Sew two remaining units together as shown to make Block 4. Press. Make two and label Block 4. Block measures 8½" square.

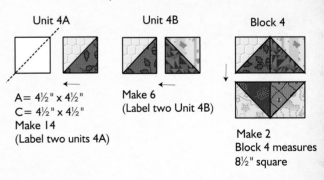

Unit 4A   Unit 4B   Block 4

A= 4½" x 4½"
C= 4½" x 4½"   Make 6
Make 14   (Label two Unit 4B)
(Label two units 4A)

Make 2
Block 4 measures
8½" square

8. Making a quick corner triangle unit, sew one 4½" Fabric B square and one 4½" Fabric A square as shown. Press. Make four. Sew these units together in pairs. Press. Make two. Sew these two units together as shown to make Block 5 and label. Block 5 measures 8½" square.

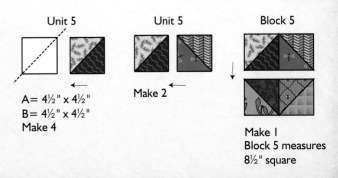

Unit 5   Unit 5   Block 5

A= 4½" x 4½"
B= 4½" x 4½"   Make 2
Make 4

Make 1
Block 5 measures
8½" square

9. Arrange and sew four different 4½" x 3½" Fabric C pieces together as shown. Press. Make forty. Label fourteen Unit 6 and set aside. Sew remaining units together as shown. Press. Make thirteen and label Block 6. Block 6 measures 12½" x 8½".

Unit 6

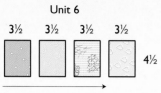

Make 40
(Label fourteen Unit 6)

Block 6

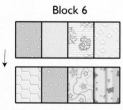

Make 13
Block 6 measures 12½"x 8½"

10. Arrange and sew three different 4½" x 3½" Fabric C pieces and one 4½" x 3½" Fabric B piece together as shown. Press. Make eight. Sew these units together in pairs as shown. Press. Make four and label Block 7. Block 7 measures 12½" x 8½".

Unit 7

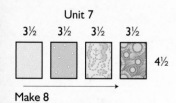

Make 8

Block 7

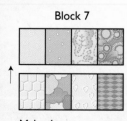

Make 4
Block 7 measures 12½"x 8½"

Assembly

Note: It is recommended that all blocks and units be arranged into Rows 1-9 prior to sewing any row to ensure a pleasing arrangement.

1. Arrange and sew the units and blocks as shown in assembly diagram on page 31 to make Rows 1-9. Press.

2. Sew rows together and press.

Making the Corner Blocks and Border

1. Sew 1¼" x 42" Fabric D strips together end-to-end to make one continuous 1¼"-wide strip. Press. Cut two 60½"-long strips. Referring to photo on page 26 and layout on page 32 sew 60½"-long strips to top and bottom of quilt. Press seams toward Fabric D. Cut two 106"-long strips and set aside.

2. Sew two 4½" x 8½" Fabric C pieces together as shown. Press. Make four.

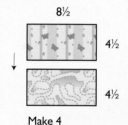

Make 4

3. Sew unit from step 2 to one 4½" x 8½" Fabric C piece as shown. Press. Make four in assorted combinations.

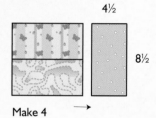

Make 4

4. Refer to Quick Corner Triangles on page 92. Making a quick corner triangle unit, sew one 4½" Fabric B square and one 4½" x 12½" Fabric C piece as shown. Press. Make twelve. Making a quick corner triangle unit, sew one 4½" Fabric A square and one 4½" x 12½" Fabric C piece as shown. Press. Make six.

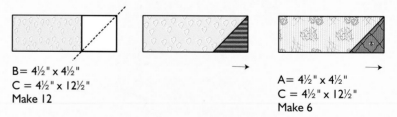

B= 4½" x 4½"
C = 4½" x 12½"
Make 12

A= 4½" x 4½"
C = 4½" x 12½"
Make 6

5. Sew one unit from step 3 to one unit from step 4 as shown. Press. Make four, two with Fabric B corners and two with Fabric A corners. Corner Block measures 12½" square.

Corner Block

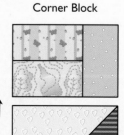

Make 4
(2 with Fabric B corners, 2 with Fabric A corners)
Corner Block measures 12½" square

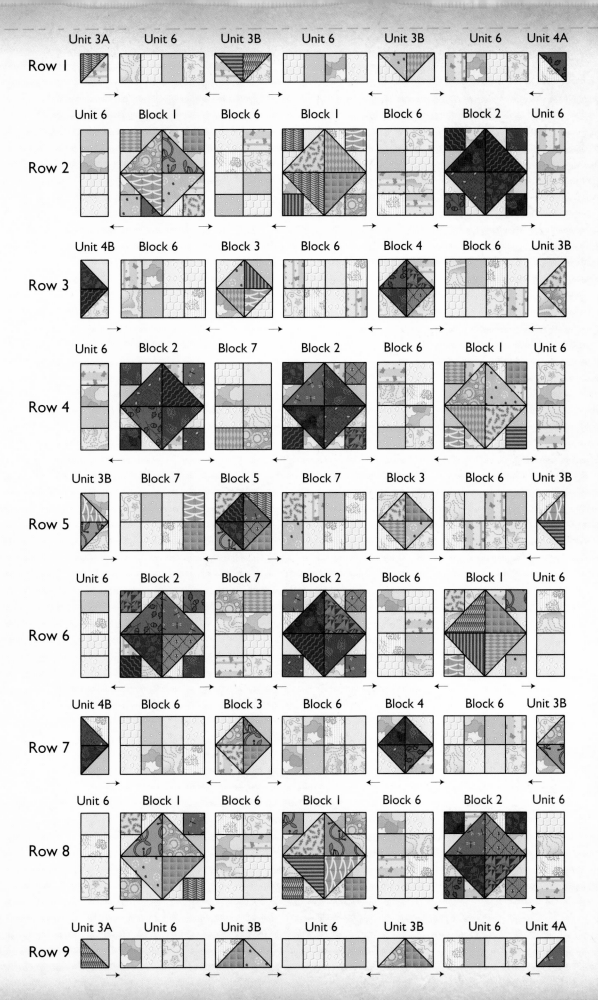

Row 1 — Unit 3A · Unit 6 · Unit 3B · Unit 6 · Unit 3B · Unit 6 · Unit 4A

Row 2 — Unit 6 · Block 1 · Block 6 · Block 1 · Block 6 · Block 2 · Unit 6

Row 3 — Unit 4B · Block 6 · Block 3 · Block 6 · Block 4 · Block 6 · Unit 3B

Row 4 — Unit 6 · Block 2 · Block 7 · Block 2 · Block 6 · Block 1 · Unit 6

Row 5 — Unit 3B · Block 7 · Block 5 · Block 7 · Block 3 · Block 6 · Unit 3B

Row 6 — Unit 6 · Block 2 · Block 7 · Block 2 · Block 6 · Block 1 · Unit 6

Row 7 — Unit 4B · Block 6 · Block 3 · Block 6 · Block 4 · Block 6 · Unit 3B

Row 8 — Unit 6 · Block 1 · Block 6 · Block 1 · Block 6 · Block 2 · Unit 6

Row 9 — Unit 3A · Unit 6 · Unit 3B · Unit 6 · Unit 3B · Unit 6 · Unit 4A

Earth and Water Bed Quilt
Finished Size: 86½" x 106½"

6. Making a quick corner triangle unit, sew one 4½" Fabric B square and one 4½" x 12½" Fabric C piece as shown. Press. Make ten. Making a quick corner triangle unit, sew one 4½" Fabric A square and one 4½" x 12½" Fabric C piece as shown. Press. Make four.

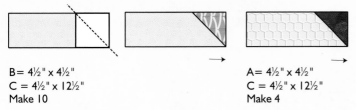

B = 4½" x 4½"
C = 4½" x 12½"
Make 10

A = 4½" x 4½"
C = 4½" x 12½"
Make 4

7. Arrange and sew four different 3½" x 12½" Fabric C pieces as shown. Press. Make fourteen in assorted combinations.

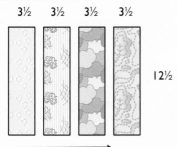

3½   3½   3½   3½

12½

Make 14 in assorted combinations

8. Arrange and sew three units from step 4, three units from step 6, and three units from step 7 as shown. Press. Sew to top of quilt. Press seam toward Accent strip.

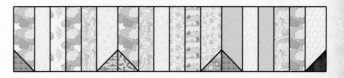

9. Repeat step 8 rearranging quick corner triangle units from steps 4 and 6 to coordinate with bottom of quilt. Sew to bottom of quilt.

10. Referring to photo on page 26 and layout, sew 106"-long Fabric D strips to sides of quilt. Press seams toward Fabric D.

11. Referring to photo on page 26 and layout, arrange and sew two Corner Blocks, two 1¼" x 12½" Fabric D strips, four units from step 6, four units from step 7, and four units from step 4, placing position of dark and medium triangles to coordinate with quilt top triangles. Press. Sew to sides of quilt. Press.

Layering and Finishing

1. Cut backing crosswise into three equal pieces. Sew pieces together to make one 96" x 120"(approximate) backing piece. Press.

2. Arrange and baste backing, batting, and top together referring to Layering the Quilt on page 94.

3. Machine or hand quilt as desired.

4. Sew 2¾"-wide binding strips end-to-end to make one continuous 2¾"-wide binding strip. Refer to Binding the Quilt on page 94 and bind quilt to finish.

Earth and Water

Fountain

Add a mosaic flowerpot fountain to your garden for an organic and unusual accent. Tumbled glass forms a stream through a rock bed on this fun to make garden accessory.

Supply List

Tin Flowerpot

Tumbled Glass Mosaic Pieces* – Blue, aqua, green, white

Glass Cutter, 3-1 Lubricating oil, Pliers, and Safety Glasses

Clear Silicone Adhesive Caulk

Premixed Ceramic Tile Adhesive and Grout – Sanded Antique White

Polished River Rocks* – Medium Size White, Medium Size Assorted, and Small Size Assorted

Decorative Glass Gems* – Iridescent light orange

Palette Knife, Sponge, Rags

Glass Mosaic Sealer

Plywood Board Cut to Fit Inside Flowerpot

Marine Varnish

Container Fountain Kit and Installation Tools

*Available at most craft stores

Getting Started

Mosaic work on this flowerpot is done in stages depending on the materials and techniques used and allowing for drying time between steps. We recommend silicone caulk for glueing the glass pieces because it dries clear, can be applied to individual pieces, and is easy to use. The premixed ceramic tile adhesive and grout is used to grout the glass pieces and as adhesive and grout (all in one step) for the rocks and gems. Use a fountain kit to make this flowerpot into a fountain, or fill it with flowering plants for a beautiful garden accent.

Making the Mosaic Flowerpot

1. Referring to photo, draw stream bed and sun on flowerpot.

2. Tumbled glass mosaic pieces come in a variety of sizes and shapes. Following the stream outline, arrange glass pieces leaving ⅛" space between pieces and varying sizes, shapes, and colors to create the stream bed. If laying glass pieces directly on the flowerpot is difficult because of a curve, make a paper pattern of the streambed and lay pieces on paper. If needed, glass can be cut to fit as described in steps 3-5.

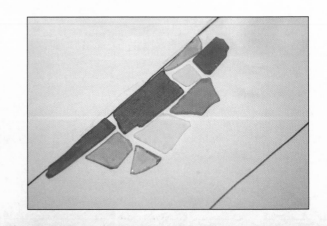

3. Cover a flat work surface with several layers of newspaper. Hold cutter the way it feels most comfortable. It is essential that the cutter is lubricated each time before scoring glass. Safety Glasses and gloves must be worn while working with glass. Stand to cut glass which allows clear sight and proper pressure while cutting. Glass is not cut, it is scored, so it doesn't take a lot of strength. Exerting comfortable pressure, the wheel of the cutter scratches the glass, creating a stress point. When pressure is applied to the score line, the glass should break along the line. When cutting stained glass, always score the glass on its smoothest side.

4. Hold glass securely against a hard surface with one gloved hand while scoring with the other. Begin to score at the edge of the glass. Maintain an even pressure while scoring. Score line should be visible and a gentle 'ripping' sound should be heard. If no sound is heard or a score line is not visible, apply more pressure with next score. A heavy, white, fuzzy line indicates that too much pressure is being used. Different types of glass will require different pressure.

5. Once the glass is scored, hold glass securely with one hand and position the jaws of the pliers parallel to, but not directly on the score line. Make a sharp upward and outward movement and the glass will break along the score line. Practice the technique several times using clear glass before cutting colored glass.

6. When satisfied with the arrangement of glass pieces, apply clear silicone caulk to the back of each individual piece, one at a time, to glue pieces to flowerpot. Allow to dry overnight.

7. Using the premixed adhesive/grout and a palette knife, spread grout over glass pieces, filling spaces between pieces. Do one section at a time as grout dries quickly. Confine grout to the glass stream bed area. Immediately, use a damp sponge to wipe over top of grout area to remove excess grout. Continue wiping grout area with sponge, rinsing sponge as needed, until tops of all glass pieces are exposed and free of grout but grout completely fills spaces between glass pieces.

Continue applying, and cleaning off grout in sections until stream bed is complete. Allow to dry completely.

8. Apply ½" thick layer of adhesive/grout to flowerpot beneath streambed as shown. Press medium size white rocks into the adhesive/grout to form the banks of the stream bed. Do one section at a time.

9. Apply ¼" thick layer of adhesive/grout under medium size rocks. Press small rocks into the adhesive/grout. Repeat steps 6 and 7 for all lower sections of flowerpot. Allow to dry.

10. Apply adhesive/grout, about ¼" thick to sun circle. Press glass gems into grout to form a circle. Allow to dry.

11. Repeat steps 8 and 9 to apply medium and small rocks to the top part of flowerpot. Use adhesive/grout to adhere glass gems to rim of flowerpot. Allow to dry thoroughly.

12. Apply mosaic sealer according to manufacturer's directions and allow to dry.

13. For fountain, cut a board to fit inside flowerpot about 3" from top. For longer life, apply several coats of marine varnish to board, following manufacturer's directions. Install pump according to manufacturer's directions. Read all of the instructions for safety and maintenance. Seal all holes with silicone caulking and place leftover rocks and gems on board for a decorative finish to fountain.

Fruit Orchard

'Fruits of our labor' is the inspiration for this charming table quilt that combines embroidered fruit motifs with log cabin blocks laid out in a 'furrows' design. If embroidery isn't an option, make this quilt with fruit appliques.

Fruit Orchard
Table Quilt

Fabric Requirements and Cutting Instructions

Read all instructions before beginning and use ¼"-wide seam allowances throughout. Read Cutting Strips and Pieces on page 92 prior to cutting fabrics.

Fruit Orchard Table Quilt Finished Size: 54½" x 54½"	FIRST CUT		SECOND CUT	
	Number of Strips or Pieces	Dimensions	Number of Pieces	Dimensions
Fabric A Embroidery Background				
⅝ yard each of two fabrics	5	9" squares from each		
⅓ yard of one fabric	4	9" squares		
⅓ yard of one fabric	2	9" squares		
Fabric B Medium Green	3*	1½" x 42"	6	1½" x 11½"
			13	1½" x 10½"
			13	1½" x 9½"
¼ yard each of six fabrics			13	1½" x 8½"
			13	1½" x 7½"
			13	1½" x 6½"
*Cut randomly to equal number listed in second cuts			7	1½" x 5½"
Fabric C Dark Green	3*	1½" x 42"	5	1½" x 11½"
			9	1½" x 10½"
			9	1½" x 9½"
¼ yard each of six fabrics			9	1½" x 8½"
			9	1½" x 7½"
			9	1½" x 6½"
*Cut randomly to equal number listed in second cuts			4	1½" x 5½"
Fabric D Light Green	3*	1½" x 42"	5	1½" x 11½"
			10	1½" x 10½"
			10	1½" x 9½"
¼ yard each of six fabrics			10	1½" x 8½"
			10	1½" x 7½"
			10	1½" x 6½"
*Cut randomly to equal number listed in second cuts			5	1½" x 5½"

BORDERS

First Border ¼ yard	5	1" x 42"		
Second Border ⅓ yard	5	1¾" x 42"		
Outside Border ¾ yard	6	3½" x 42"		
Binding ½ yard	6	2¾" x 42"		

Backing - 3½ yards
Batting - 63" x 63"

Getting Started

This charming table quilt consists of sixteen log cabin blocks arranged in the Straight Furrows design. Blocks measure 11½" square (unfinished) and can be sewn quickly using an assembly line method. Block centers are embroidered on 9" squares using The Good Life by Debbie Mumm® Embroidery Card by Bernina® and then trimmed to block center size 5½" square. As an alternative, fruit motifs can be appliquéd to center squares or fussy cut fruit motifs from fruit-patterned fabric. Each shade of log consists of six fabrics which add movement and interest to the quilt.

To simplify and speed the cutting process and provide variety within the blocks, the 1½" x 42" Fabric B strips were stacked in assorted layers 3 or 4 fabrics deep. Strip lengths were then cut starting with the largest size continuing with diminishing sizes (11½", 10½", 9½", etc.) until the required number of pieces were cut. The same procedure was followed for Fabrics C and D.

Refer to Accurate Seam Allowance on page 92. Whenever possible, use the Assembly Line Method on page 92. Press seams in direction of arrows.

Making the Blocks

1. Embroider (or appliqué) four pears, two lemons, five apples, and five plums on 9" Fabric A squares. Cut a template using cardboard or a similar material with a 5½" square opening. Place template over one fruit embroidery to visually center design as shown. Mark the desired position with a temporary marker. Using square ruler and rotary cutter, cut on drawn lines. Make sixteen, one for each embroidered piece.

2. Sew one 1½" x 5½" Fabric B strip to top of one 5½" pear embroidery square from step 1 as shown. Press. Make five, four pears and one lemon.

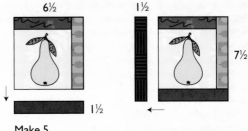

Make 5
(4 with pears, 1 with lemon)

3. Sew one 1½" x 6½" Fabric B strip to side of unit from step 2 as shown. Press. Make five, four pears and one lemon.

Make 5
(4 with pears, 1 with lemon)

4. Sew one 1½" x 6½" Fabric C strip to bottom of unit from step 3 as shown. Press. Sew one 1½" x 7½" Fabric C strip to side of unit as shown. Make five, four pears and one lemon.

Make 5
(4 with pears, 1 with lemon)

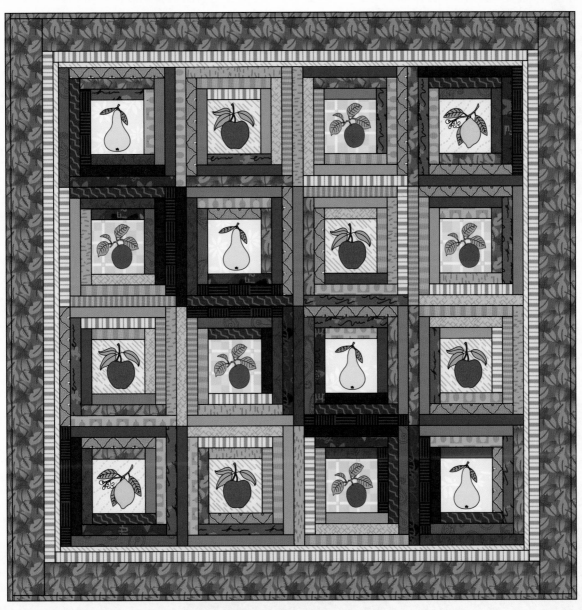

Fruit Orchard Table Quilt
Finished Size: 54½" x 54½"

5. Sew one 1½" x 7½" Fabric B strip to top of unit from step 4 as shown. Press. Sew one 1½" x 8½" Fabric B strip to side of unit as shown. Press. Make five, four pears and one lemon.

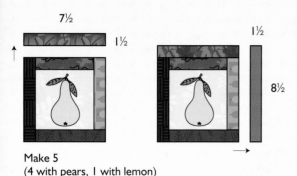

Make 5
(4 with pears, 1 with lemon)

6. Sew one 1½" x 8½" Fabric C strip to bottom of unit from step 5 as shown. Press. Sew one 1½" x 9½" Fabric C strip to side of unit as shown. Make five, four pears and one lemon.

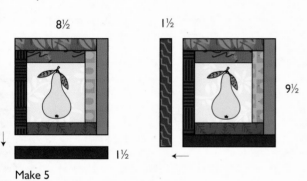

Make 5
(4 with pears, 1 with lemon)

7. Sew one 1½" x 9½" Fabric B strip to top of unit from step 6 as shown. Press. Sew one 1½" x 10½" Fabric B strip to side of unit as shown. Press. Make five, four pears and one lemon.

Make 5
(4 with pears, 1 with lemon)

8. Sew one 1½" x 10½" Fabric C strip to bottom of unit from step 7 as shown. Press. Sew one 1½" x 11½" Fabric C strip to side as shown. Press. Make five, four pears and one lemon. Block One measures 11½" square.

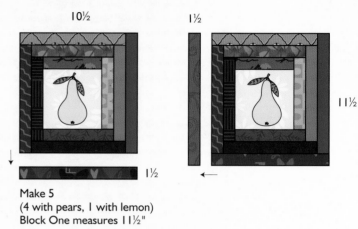

Make 5
(4 with pears, 1 with lemon)
Block One measures 11½"

9. Referring to steps 2-8, sew Fabric D and Fabric B strips to 5½" apple embroidery squares as shown starting with Fabric D. Make five. Block Two measures 11½" square.

Make 5
Block Two measures 11½"

10. Referring to steps 2-8, sew Fabric B and Fabric D strips to 5½" plum embroidery squares as shown starting with Fabric B. Make two. Block Three measures 11½" square.

Make 2
Block Three measures 11½"

11. Referring to steps 2-8, sew Fabric C and Fabric B strips to one 5½" lemon embroidery square as shown starting with Fabric C. Make one. Block Four measures 11½" square.

Make 1
Block Four measures 11½"

12. Referring to steps 2-8, sew Fabric C and Fabric D strips to 5½" plum embroidery squares as shown starting with Fabric C. Make three. Block Five measures 11½" square.

Make 3
Block Five measures 11½"

Assembly

1. Referring to photo on page 36 and layout on page 39, arrange and sew Blocks One, Two, Three, and Four together to make row one. Press seams in one direction.

2. Referring to photo on page 36 and layout on page 39, arrange and sew Blocks Five, One, Two, and Three, to make row two. Press seams in the opposite direction from row one. On the blocks re-press the 1½" x 11½" strip so the seams will be in the opposite direction from the seams on row one. Sew rows one and two together.

3. Referring to photo and layout, arrange and sew the last two remaining rows of blocks together Blocks Two, Three, One and Two to make Row Three. Sew together Blocks One, Two, Three, and One to make Row 4. Re-pressing seams as needed. Sew these rows to row unit from step 2. Press.

Adding the Borders

1. Sew 1" x 42" First Border strips together end-to-end to make one continuous 1"-wide First Border strip. Press. Referring to Adding the Borders on page 94, measure quilt through center from side to side. Cut two 1"-wide First Border strips to this measurement. Sew to top and bottom of quilt. Press seams toward border.

2. Measure quilt through center from top to bottom including borders just added. Cut two 1"-wide First Border strips to this measurement. Sew to sides of quilt. Press.

3. Refer to steps 1 and 2 to join, measure, trim, and sew 1¾" Second Border and 3½"-wide Outside Border strips to top, bottom, and sides of quilt. Press.

Layering and Finishing

1. Cut backing crosswise into two equal pieces. Sew pieces together to make one 63" x 80" (approximate) backing piece. Press and trim to 63" x 63".

2. Arrange and baste backing, batting, and top together referring to Layering the Quilt on page 94.

3. Machine or hand quilt as desired.

4. Sew 2¾"-wide binding strips end-to-end to make one continuous 2¾"-wide binding strip. Refer to Binding the Quilt on page 94 and bind quilt to finish.

Materials Needed for One Placemat

Fabric A (Embroidery Background) – One 9" square piece

Fabric B (Medium Green) – Assorted Scraps

Fabric D (Light Green) – Assorted Scraps

**Cut one each of Fabric B and Fabric D in the following sizes

      1½" x 13½" (Fabric B only)

      1½" x 12½"

      1½" x 11½"

      1½" x 10½"

      1½" x 9½"

      1½" x 8½"

      1½" x 7½"

      1½" x 6½"

      1½" x 5½" (Fabric D only)

Border and Binding – ¼ yard

      Two 3½" x 13½" Pieces

      Two 2¾" x 42" Strips

Fruit Orchard Placemat
Finished Size: 20" x 14"

Making the Placemat

1. Referring to Making the Blocks, steps 1-9, on pages 38-40, make one 11½" square apple block, Block Two.

2. Sew 1½" x 11½" and 1½" x 12½" Fabric D strips to top and right sides of block. Sew 1½" x 12½" and 1½" x 13½" Fabric B strips to bottom and left sides of block. Block measures 13½" square.

3. Sew 3½" x 13½" Fabric B pieces to each side of block.

4. Arrange and baste backing, batting and placemat top together referring to Layering the Quilt on page 94.

5. Machine or hand quilt as desired.

6. Refer to Binding the Quilt on page 94 and bind placemat to finish.

"An apple a day" takes on new meaning when you start each day with this fruit-centered placemat. Use leftover strips from the Fruit Orchard Table Quilt to make a whole set of charming placemats.

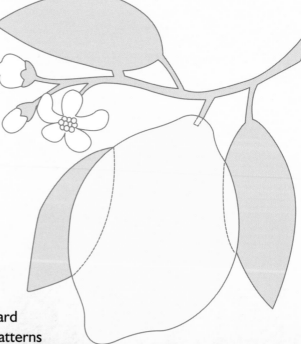

Fruit Orchard
Appliqué Patterns

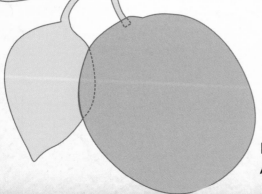

Orchard Potholders

Fruit Orchard Potholders
Finished Size: 6½" x 11½"

Complete your kitchen ensemble with handsome and handy leaf potholders.

Tracing Line	———————
Tracing Line	-----------------------------
(Will be hidden behind other fabrics)	

Leaf Potholders

Use green fabric scraps and batting to make these quick and cute potholders.

1. Enlarge whole leaf pattern on page 17 to 125%.

2. Using pattern, cut two matching leaf shapes for each potholder.

3. Place two fabric leaf pieces, right sides together, and place on batting scrap.

4. Using ¼"-wide seams, sew around leaf shape, leaving a 3" opening for turning. Trim batting close to stitches and turn leaf right side out. Press. Hand-sew opening closed and press.

5. Quilt as desired.

6. Cut two matching stems using fabric scraps and Leaf Potholder Stem Pattern.

7. Press edges under ¼" on all sides.

8. Referring to photo, place pressed stem piece on each side of quilted leaf shape, pin, lining up stem pieces. Top-stitch in place, securing bottom pieces of stems by sewing stem pieces together.

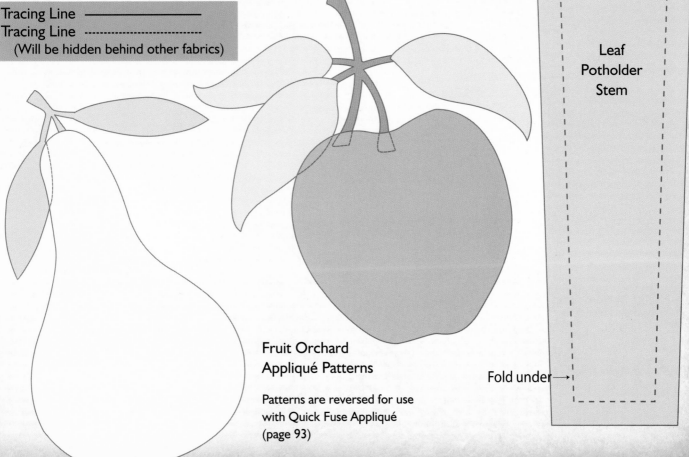

Leaf Potholder Stem

Fold under →

Fruit Orchard Appliqué Patterns

Patterns are reversed for use with Quick Fuse Appliqué (page 93)

Americana

Reminiscent of early America, this heartwarming quilt uses vintage-look fabrics and a scrappy design to present patriotic appeal perfect for a garden quilt. Used on a picnic table or hung from a barn, this quilt is as American as apple pie.

Americana
Bed Quilt

Americana Bed Quilt Finished Size: 77" x 93"	FIRST CUT		SECOND CUT	
	Number of Strips or Pieces	Dimensions	Number of Pieces	Dimensions
Fabric A Light Tan Background and Squares ⅝ yard each of four fabrics *Cut for each fabric	1* 1* 1**	9" x 42" 8½" x 42" 2½" x 42" **(cut from two fabrics only)	2* 3* 10**	9" squares (cut once diagonally) 8½" squares 2½" squares** **(cut from two fabrics only)
Fabric B Medium Tan Background and Squares ⅜ yard each of four fabrics *Cut for each fabric	2* 1*	4½" x 42" 2½" x 42"	1* 13* 16*	4½" x 8½" 4½" squares 2½" squares
Fabric C Light Brown Strips and Squares ⅙ yard each of two fabrics *Cut for each fabric	2*	2" x 42"		
Fabric D Dark Brown Strips and Squares ½ yard each of four fabrics *Cut for each fabric	1* 1* 4*	4½" x 42" 2½" x 42" 2" x 42"	3* 11*	4½" squares 2½" squares
Fabric E Blue Strips and Squares ⅓ yard each of three fabrics *Cut for each fabric	1* 3*	2½" x 42" 2" x 42"	8*	2½" squares
Fabric F Red Triangles and Squares ⅓ yard each of eight fabrics *Cut for each fabric	1*	9½" x 42"	2* 3*	9½" squares (cut twice diagonally) 2½" squares

Americana Quilt Continued	FIRST CUT	
	Number of Strips or Pieces	Dimensions
BORDERS		
First Border ⅜ yard	8	1½" x 42"
Second Border ⅓ yard	8	1" x 42"
Outside Border 1¼ yard	8	5" x 42"
Binding ¾ yard	9	2¾" x 42"
Backing - 7⅛ yards Batting - 85" x 101" Template Plastic (optional)		

This heartwarming quilt echoes many designs popular throughout American quilt history. Variations on two blocks, Diamond and Cross-Hatch, are incorporated in the quilt. The warm palette of red, blue, gold, and tan is a centuries old favorite.

Getting Started

Blocks measure 16½" square unfinished. This quilt gets its charm with a scrap look, but note how background pieces (Fabric B) match within the squares.

Refer to Accurate Seam Allowance on page 92. Whenever possible, use the Assembly Line Method on page 92. Press seams in direction of arrows.

Fabric Requirements and Cutting Instructions

Read all instructions before beginning and use ¼"-wide seam allowances throughout. Read Cutting Strips and Pieces on page 92 prior to cutting fabrics.

Making the Diamond Block

1. Arrange and sew a combination of four 2" x 42" Fabric C, D, or E strips together as shown to make a strip set. Press. Make seven sets in assorted combinations.

42

2
2
2
2

Make 7 sets
(in assorted C,D,E combinations)

2. Cut a 9" square template from template plastic, poster board or a similar material. Cut square in half diagonally.

9

Template

9

3. Using the template from step 2, mark and cut five triangles from each strip set as shown to make a total of thirty-two triangles.

Cut 32
(5 from each strip set)

Americana Bed Quilt
Finished Size: 77" x 93"

4. Sew one Fabric A triangle to one triangle unit from step 3 as shown. Press. Square to 8½". Make eight. Sew these units together in pairs. Press. Make four.

Make 4 →

Make 8
(in assorted combinations)
Square to 8½"

5. Sew two different Fabric F triangles together as shown. Press. Make thirty-two units in assorted combinations.

→

Make 32
(in assorted combinations)

6. Sew one triangle unit from step 5 to one triangle unit from step 3 as shown. Press. Square to 8½". Make twenty-four. Sew these units together in pairs as shown. Press. Make twelve.

Make 12 ←

Make 24
(in assorted combinations)
square to 8½"

7. Sew one unit from step 4 to one unit from step 6 as shown. Press. Make four and label Diamond Block One. Sew two units from step 6 together as shown. Press. Make four and label Diamond Block Two. Blocks measure 16½" square.

Diamond Block One

Make 4
Diamond Block One measures
16½" square

Diamond Block Two

Make 4
Diamond Block Two measures
16½" square

Making the Cross-Hatch Block

1. Sew one 2½" Fabric B square and one 2½" Fabric D square together as shown. Press. Continue sewing one 2½" Fabric B square to one 2½" Fabric D, E, or F square as shown to make a total of sixty-four units. We used sixty-four Fabric B squares with thirty-five 2½" Fabric D squares, seventeen 2½" Fabric E squares, and twelve 2½" Fabric F squares.

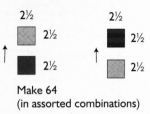

Make 64
(in assorted combinations)

2. Sew units from step 1 together in pairs as shown matching Fabric B colors. Press. Make thirty-two.

←

Make 32
(in assorted combinations)

3. Sew one matching 4½" Fabric B square to one unit from step 2 as shown. Press. Make thirty-two, matching Fabric B pieces.

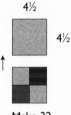

Make 32
(in assorted combinations)

4. Sew two units from step 3 together as shown, matching Fabric B pieces. Press. Make eight.

→

Make 8
(in assorted combinations)

5. Sew two units from step 4 together as shown. Press. Make four and label Unit 1.

Unit 1

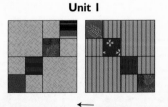

Make 4
(in assorted combinations)

6. Sew two 8½" Fabric A squares together as shown. Press. Make six and label Unit 2.

Unit 2

8½   8½

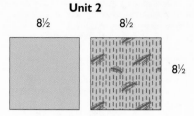

8½

Make 6
(in assorted combinations)

7. Sew one Unit 2 from step 6 to one Unit 1 from step 5 as shown. Press. Make two. Cross-Hatch Block One measures 16½" square.

Cross-Hatch One

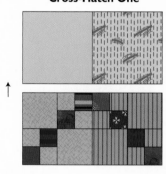

Make 2
Cross-Hatch One measures 16½" square

8. Sew one 4½" Fabric B square to one 4½" Fabric D square as shown. Press. Make ten and label Unit 3. Sew this unit to one matching 4½" x 8½" Fabric B piece as shown. Press. Make four and label Unit 4.

Unit 3   **Unit 4**

4½   8½

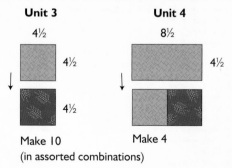

4½   4½

4½   4½

Make 10   Make 4
(in assorted combinations)

9. Sew one 2½" Fabric A square to one 2½" Fabric D, E, or F square as shown. Press. Make twenty in assorted A/D, A/E, and A/F combinations. Sew these units together in pairs as shown. Make ten.

2½

2½

2½

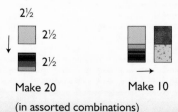

Make 20   Make 10
(in assorted combinations)

10. Sew one 4½" Fabric B square to one unit from step 9 as shown. Press. Make ten in assorted combinations.

4½

4½

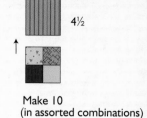

Make 10
(in assorted combinations)

11. Sew one unit from step 10 to one unit from step 3 matching Fabric B pieces as shown. Press. Make ten in assorted combinations.

Make 10
(in assorted combinations and matching background Fabric B)

12. Sew one Unit 3 from step 8 to one unit from step 3 matching Fabric B pieces as shown. Press. Make six in assorted combinations.

Make 6
(in assorted combinations and matching background Fabric B)

13. Sew one Unit 4 from step 8 to one unit from step 11 as shown. Press. Make four in assorted combinations.

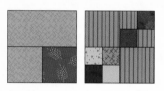

Make 4
(in assorted combinations)

14. Sew one unit from step 11 to one unit from step 12 as shown. Press. Make six in assorted combinations.

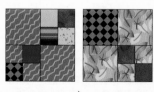

Make 6
(in assorted combinations)

15. Sew one unit from step 13 to one unit from step 14 as shown. Press. Make four. Cross-Hatch Block Two measures 16½" square.

Cross-Hatch Block Two

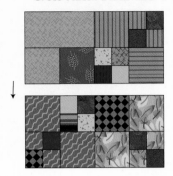

Make 4
Cross-Hatch Block Two measures 16½" square

16. Sew two units from step 14 together as shown. Press Cross-Hatch Block Three measures 16½" square.

Cross-Hatch Block Three

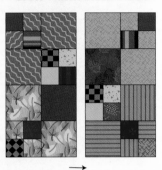

Cross-Hatch Block Three measures 16½" square

Assembly

1. Sew one Fabric A triangle to one Fabric F unit (Making the Diamond Block, step 5) as shown. Press. Square to 8½". Make eight. Sew two of these units together as shown. Press. Make four and label Unit 5.

 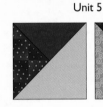

Unit 5

Make 8
(in assorted combinations)
Square to 8½"

Make 4

2. Referring to photo on page 44 and layout on page 47, arrange and sew together two of Unit 2, two of Diamond Block One and one of Cross-Hatch Block One to make a row. Press. Make two rows.

3. Arrange and sew together two of Unit 5, two of Cross-Hatch Block Two and one Diamond Block Two to make a row. Press. Make two.

4. Arrange and sew together two of Unit 1, two of Diamond Block Two, and Cross-Hatch Block Three to make a row. Press.

5. Referring to photo on page 44 and layout on page 47, arrange and sew rows from steps 1, 2, and 3 together. Press seams in one direction.

Adding the Borders

1. Sew 1½" x 42" First Border strips together end-to-end to make one continuous 1½"-wide First Border strip. Press. Referring to Adding the Borders on page 94, measure quilt through center from side to side. Cut two 1½"-wide border strips to this measurement. Sew to top and bottom of quilt. Press seams toward border.

2. Measure quilt through center from top to bottom including borders just added. Cut two 1½"-wide First Border strips to this measurement. Sew to sides of quilt. Press.

3. Refer to steps 1 and 2 to join, measure, trim, and sew 1"-wide Second Border and 5"-wide Outside Border strips to top, bottom, and sides of quilt. Press.

Layering and Finishing

1. Cut backing crosswise into three equal pieces. Sew pieces together to make one 85" x 120" (approximate) backing piece. Press and trim to 85" x 101".

2. Arrange and baste backing, batting, and top together referring to Layering the Quilt on page 94.

3. Machine or hand quilt as desired.

4. Sew 2¾"-wide binding strips end-to-end to make one continuous 2¾"-wide binding strip. Refer to Binding the Quilt on page 94 and bind quilt to finish.

Americana
Stars

Rustic wooden stars make a patriotic statement in the garden when mounted on a fence or attached to stakes in a flower bed. The stars are easy to make and will add a touch of Americana to any setting.

Supply List

Large Star:
Five ¼" x 1" Boards Cut into 18" Lengths
Delta Ceramcoat® Acrylic Paint - Tompte Red

Small Star:
Five ¼" x 1" Boards Cut into 12" Lengths
Americana® Acrylic Paint – Golden Straw

Needed for either Star
FolkArt® Antiquing Medium by Plaid®
    - Woodn' Bucket Brown
Assorted Small Screws
Paintbrushes
Sandpaper
Exterior Spray Matte Varnish

Making the Stars

1. Arrange boards together as shown into a star shape. Screw together at points. If screws are too long, cut off the ends and sand smooth.

2. Paint large star with Tompte Red paint. Paint small star with Golden Straw. Two coats may be needed for good coverage. Allow to dry overnight.

3. Distress wooden stars by sanding the edges creating faux "wear spots." Remove sanding residue.

4. Apply antiquing medium to star, wiping off or adding antiquing medium until the desired look is achieved. When dry, spray with exterior matte varnish.

Watermelon
Make 3

Watermelon Appliqué Pattern
Tracing Line ———————
Tracing Line ----------------------
(will be hidden behind other fabric)
Placement Line -·-·-·-·-·-·-·-

Watermelon
Wallhanging

Watermelon Wallhanging Finished Size: 33" x 22"	FIRST CUT		SECOND CUT	
	Number of Strips or Pieces	Dimensions	Number of Pieces	Dimensions
Fabric A Pinwheel Background 1/8 yard each of three fabrics *Cut for each fabric	1*	3½" x 42"	8*	3½" squares
Fabric B Pinwheel 1/8 yard each of three fabrics *Cut for each fabric	1*	3½" x 42"	8*	3½" squares
Fabric C Appliqué Background 1/4 yard each of three fabrics *Cut for each fabric	1*	6½" x 16½"		
Fabric D Accent Border 1/8 yard	1	1" x 42"	2	1" x 18½"
BORDERS				
First Border 1/8 yard	3	1" x 42"	2 2	1" x 29½" 1" x 19½"
Outside Border 1/4 yard	4	1½" x 42"	2 2	1½" x 30½" 1½" x 21½"
Binding 3/8 yard	4	2¾" x 42"		

Backing - ¾ yard
Batting - 37" x 26"
Watermelon Appliqués - 1/8 yard each of three fabrics
Rind Appliqués - 1/8 yard each of three fabrics
Lightweight Fusible Web - 1 yard
Black Beads or Buttons - 33

Fabric Requirements and Cutting Instructions

Read all instructions before beginning and use ¼"-wide seam allowances throughout. Read Cutting Strips and Pieces on page 92 prior to cutting fabrics.

Pinwheels and watermelons- the perfect way to celebrate summer. Watermelons are appliquéd and embellished with bead watermelon seeds. For directional fabrics, such as stripes, note direction when sewing quick corner triangles.

Watermelon Wallhanging
Finished Size: 33" x 22"

Getting Started

Pinwheel Blocks measure 6½" square (unfinished). Refer to Accurate Seam Allowance on page 92 and use ¼" wide seams throughout. Whenever possible, use the Assembly Line Method on page 92. Press seams in direction of arrows.

Making the Quilt Top

1. Refer to Quick Corner Triangles on page 92. Making a quick corner triangle, sew one 3½" Fabric A square and one 3½" Fabric B square together as shown. Press. Make twenty-four, eight of each combination.

A=3½" x 3½"
B=3½" x 3½"
Make 24
(8 of each combination)

2. Sew two matching units from step 1 together as shown. Press. Make twelve, four of each combination.

Make 12
(4 of each combination)

3. Sew two matching units from step 2 together as shown. Press. Make six, two of each combination. Block measures 6½" square. See Twisting Seams Tip on page 88 for center pressing.

Make 6
(2 of each combination)
Block measures 6½" square

4. Sew three blocks from step 3 together as shown. Press. Make two.

Make 2 →   →

5. Sew three 6½" x 16½" Fabric C pieces together as shown. Press.

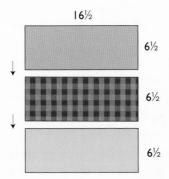

16½

6½

6½

6½

6. Sew units from step 4, two 1" x 18½" Fabric D strips, and unit from step 5 together as shown. Press.

1   1

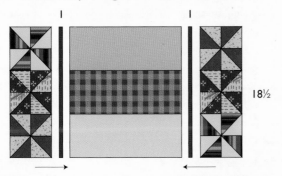

18½

7. Sew two 1" x 29½" First Border strips to top and bottom of quilt. Press. Sew two 1" x 19½" First Border strips to sides. Press.

8. Sew two 1½" x 30½" Outside border strips to top and bottom of quilt. Press. Sew two 1½" x 21½" strips to sides. Press.

Adding the Appliqués

Refer to appliqué instructions on page 93. Our instructions are for Quick-Fuse Appliqué. If you prefer hand appliqué, add ¼"-wide seam allowances to patterns.

1. Using Watermelon Pattern on page 51, trace onto pattern paper including placement line. Fold paper along placement line and using a light box or window, trace reverse image of pattern to make a whole watermelon slice. Use this new pattern to trace three melons and three rinds on paper side of fusible web. Use assorted appliqué fabrics to prepare appliqués for fusing.

2. Referring to photo and layout, position and fuse appliqués to quilt. Finish appliqué edges with machine satin stitch or other decorative stitching as desired.

Layering and Finishing

1. Cut backing into 37" x 26" piece.

2. Arrange and baste backing, batting, and top together referring to Layering the Quilt on page 94.

3. Hand or machine quilt as desired.

4. Refer to Binding the Quilt on page 94 and bind quilt to finish.

5. Referring to photo on page 45 and layout to arrange and sew beads or buttons to watermelon appliqués.

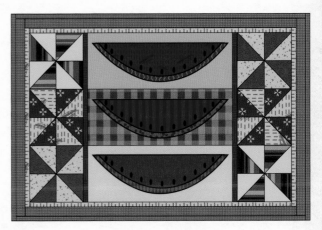

Watermelon Wallhanging
Finished Size: 33" x 22"

Sunflowers

With its face to the sun, this sunflower catches and reflects the light making a unique and beautiful garden ornament. Colored glass and half-round gems are adhered to a vintage window to make this eye-catching accessory.

Sunflower
Window

Hanging from a porch roof or mounted in the middle of the garden on a fence post, this fun garden art will sparkle and shine, adding a surprising touch of whimsy wherever it's placed. Colored glass and half-round gems create the sunflower on this eye-catching accessory.

Sunflower Window
Finished Size: 18" x 28"

Supply List

Vintage Window (Ours is 18" x 28")

Colored Glass in a Variety of Textures and Hues – Red, gold/yellow, green, brown

Decorative Gems – Clear, light blue, medium blue, opalescent, red and orange in various sizes.

Clear Kitchen & Bath Adhesive Caulk – 5.5 Fl. Oz. Tube

Glass Cutter

Lubricating Oil

Glass Pliers

Safety Goggles

Gloves

Paper and Pencil

Making the Pattern

1. Cut a piece of paper to the size of glass in window. Using patterns on page 58 as a guide, draw a pattern for sunflower on paper as shown. Enlarge or decrease sizes of petals, center, and leaves to fit your window. Draw stem and leaf veins. This drawing will be a basic guideline for sizes and shapes, but it is not necessary to follow it exactly when cutting glass.

Cutting Glass

1. Cover a flat work surface with several layers of newspaper. Hold cutter however it feels most comfortable. It is essential that the cutter is lubricated each time before scoring glass.

2. Safety Glasses and gloves must be worn while working with glass. Stand to score glass which allows clear sight and proper pressure while scoring. Glass is not cut, it is scored, so it doesn't take a lot of strength. By exerting firm but comfortable pressure, the wheel of the cutter scratches the glass, creating a stress point. When pressure is applied to the score line, the glass should break along the line. When cutting colored glass, always score the glass on its smoothest side.

3. On padded surface, hold glass securely with one gloved hand while scoring with the other. Begin to score at the edge of the glass. Maintain an even pressure while scoring. Score line should be visible and a gentle 'ripping' sound should be heard. If no sound is heard or a score line isn't seen, apply more pressure with the next score. A heavy, white, fuzzy line indicates that too much pressure is being used. Different types of glass will require different pressure.

4. Once the glass is scored, hold glass securely with one hand and position the jaws of the pliers parallel to, but not directly on the score line. Make a sharp upward and outward movement and the glass will break along the score line. Practice the technique several times using clear glass scraps before cutting colored glass.

5. Using the pattern as a general guideline, cut petals from yellow and gold glass. Cut a variety of green glass into small pieces to make the leaves. Cut brown glass into long, narrow strips for stem and veins; and cut red glass into small pieces to use in flower center.

6. Place paper pattern under window glass, facing up. Place cut glass pieces on window as indicated by the pattern. If needed re-cut pieces to fit well into a mosaic pattern on leaves.

7. Fill in flower center with orange and red decorative gems and cut red glass. When satisfied with the arrangement, begin to glue each piece of glass to the window using the clear adhesive caulk. Put caulk on back of each piece then position on window. Glue the petals, then stem and leaves before doing the background.

8. Add decorative gems in clear, opalescent, light blue, and medium blue to the background, securing each gem with clear adhesive caulk.

9. Allow window to dry several days before hanging as desired. Edges of stained glass will be sharp, so be sure to hang window out of reach of small children. The window is also very heavy – use appropriate hangers to support the heavy weight of the project.

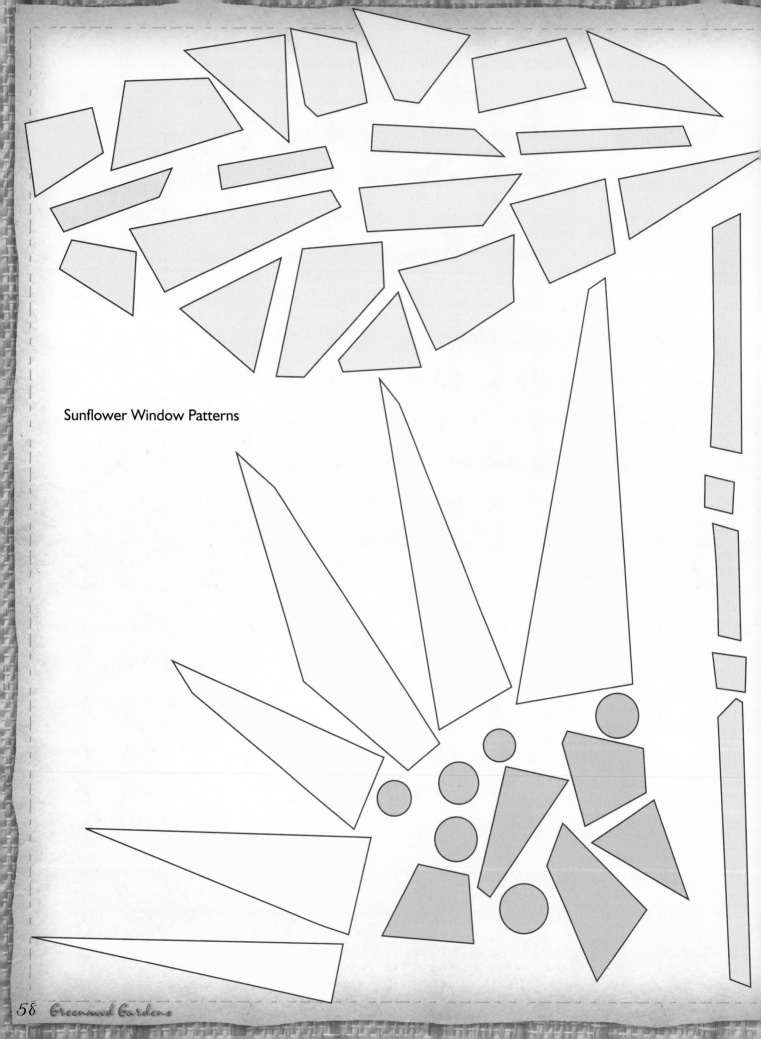

Sunflower Window Patterns

Garden Art
Ideas

The same techniques used for the Sunflower Window can be used for other themes and on other glass objects. Here two vintage windows show the use of cut glass and decorative gems to achieve very different themes and moods. The Vineyard Window features glass tiles, a cut cork, and a decoupaged wine label. Fish characters from a stained glass book were reinterpreted in the whimsical aquarium scene. A clear glass vase becomes an extraordinary accessory when a glass butterfly takes flight. Wire antenna add to this fanciful accessory. Have fun creating charming garden accents with this easy technique!

Pansy Patches

Orderly patches of pansy-hued fabrics make a garden of joyful color and texture in this sweet lap quilt. Simple nine-patch blocks get new interest by using fabrics of the same hue while sashing and borders complete the well-balanced design.

Pansy Patches

Lap Quilt

Pansy Patches Lap Quilt Finished Size: 50½"x 58½"	FIRST CUT		SECOND CUT	
	Number of Strips or Pieces	Dimensions	Number of Pieces	Dimensions
Fabric A Yellow and Purple Blocks ⅛ yard each of **nine** fabrics for each color (Three light, medium and dark of each color) *Cut for each fabric	1*	2½" x 42"	1*	2½" x 21"
Fabric B Blue and Red Blocks ⅛ yard each of **nine** fabrics for each color (Three light, medium and dark of each color) *Cut for each fabric	1*	2½" x 42"	1*	2½" x 19"
Fabric C Sashing 1⅛ yards	14	2½" x 42"	7 24	2½" x 38½ " 2½" x 6½ "
BORDERS				
First Border ¼ yard	5	1¼" x 42"		
Second Border ⅓ yard	5	1½" x 42"		
Outside Border ½ yard	6	2½" x 42"		
Binding ⅝ yard	6	2¾" x 42"		

Beautiful tonal fabrics and strip-piecing make this a sweet and speedy project. Strip sets are constructed using light, medium, and dark fabric in each colorway. Strip sets are rearranged in block assembly to give the quilt a more complex look.

Fabric Requirements and Cutting Instructions

Read all instructions before beginning and use ¼"-wide seam allowances throughout. Read Cutting Strips and Pieces on page 92 prior to cutting fabrics.

Getting Started

Refer to Accurate Seam Allowance on page 92. Whenever possible, use the Assembly Line Method on page 92. Press seams in direction of arrows. Blocks measure 6½" square unfinished.

Making the Blocks

1. Arrange and sew together three 2½" x 21" Fabric A strips (light, medium, and dark). Press. Make six sets, three in yellow and three in purple. Label strip sets 1, 2, 3. From each strip set, cut eight 2½"-wide segments as shown.

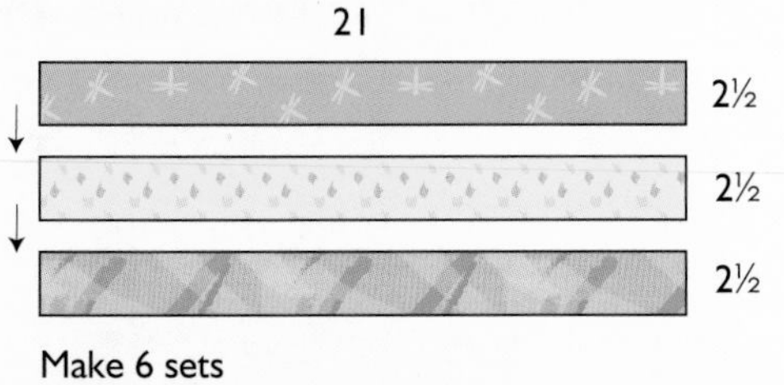

Make 6 sets
(3 in yellow, 3 in purple)

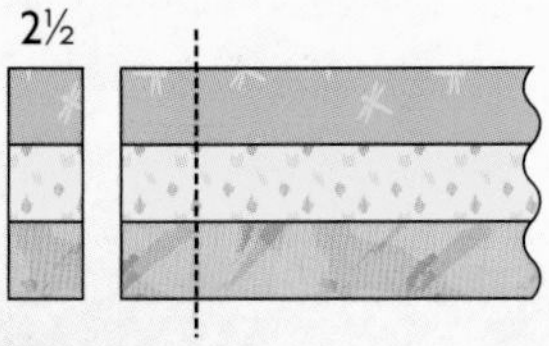

Cut 8 segments from each strip set

2. Arrange and sew three 2½" segments, one from each strip set, as shown, re-pressing any seams if needed prior to sewing. Press. Arrange remaining segments, one from each strip-set, into nine-patch blocks. Sew segments together and press. Make sixteen, eight in yellow and eight in purple.
Block measures 6½" square.

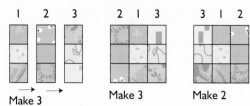

Make 3 → →   Make 3   Make 2

Make 16 assorted blocks
(8 in yellow, 8 in purple)
Blocks measure 6½" square

3. Arrange and sew together three 2½" x 19" Fabric B strips (light, medium, and dark). Press. Make six sets, three in blue and three in red. Label each color set 1, 2, 3. From each strip set, cut seven 2½"-wide segments.

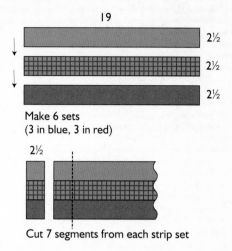

Make 6 sets
(3 in blue, 3 in red)

Cut 7 segments from each strip set

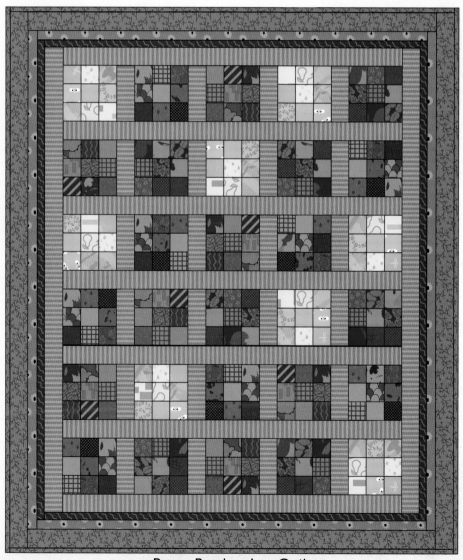

Pansy Patches Lap Quilt
Finished Size: 50½" x 58½"

4. Arrange and sew three 2½" segments from step 3, one from each strip set, as shown, re-pressing any seams if needed prior to sewing. Press. Arrange remaining segments, one from each strip-set, into nine-patch units. Sew segments together and press. Make fourteen blocks, seven in blue and seven in red. Block measures 6½" square.

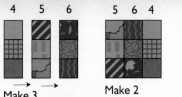

Make 3   Make 2   Make 2

Make 14 assorted blocks
(7 in red, 7 in blue)
Blocks measure 6½" square

Assembly

1. Referring to photo on page 60 and layout on page 63, arrange and sew five blocks and four 2½" x 6 ½" Fabric C pieces as shown to make a row. Press. Make six rows varying block arrangement.

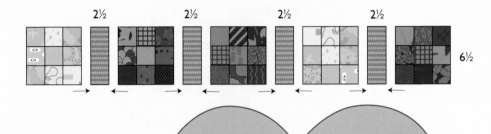

2. Referring to photo on page 60 and layout on page 63, arrange and sew seven 2½" x 38½" Fabric C strips and rows from step 1 together. Press seams toward Fabric C.

3. Sew remaining 2½" x 42" Fabric C strips end-to-end to make one continuous 2½"-wide strip. Cut two 50½"-long strips. Sew to sides of quilt. Press.

Adding the Borders

1. Sew 1¼" x 42" First Border strips together end-to-end to make one continuous 1¼"-wide First Border strip. Press. Referring to Adding the Borders on page 94, measure quilt through center from side to side. Cut two 1¼"-wide border strips to this measurement. Sew to top and bottom of quilt. Press seams toward border.

2. Measure quilt through center from top to bottom including borders just added. Cut two 1¼"-wide First Border strips to this measurement. Sew to sides of quilt. Press.

3. Refer to steps 1 and 2 to join, measure, trim, and sew 1½"-wide Second Border and 2½"-wide Outside Border strips to top, bottom, and sides of quilt. Press.

Layering and Finishing

1. Cut backing crosswise into two equal pieces. Sew pieces together to make one 57" x 80"(approximate) backing piece. Press and trim to 57" x 65".

2. Arrange and baste backing, batting, and top together referring to Layering the Quilt on page 94.

3. Machine or hand quilt as desired.

4. Sew 2¾"-wide binding strips together end-to-end to make one continuous 2¾"-wide binding strip. Refer to Binding the Quilt on page 94 and bind quilt to finish.

Pansy Patches Seed
Container Pattern

Pansy Patches
Seed Container

Store your seeds in a cute and colorful tin container that's as attractive as it is useful. An easy stamping technique creates the perky pansies and your seeds will stay dry and organized in the air-tight tin.

Supplies Needed

Tin Canister (Sides of our canister are 5½" x 8")
White Vinegar
Spray Metal Primer
Miracle Sponge™*
Delta Ceramcoat® Acrylic Paint – Crocus Yellow, Lavender, Vintage Wine, Tompte Red
Americana® Acrylic Paint – Antique Gold, Hauser Green Light, Hauser Green Dark
Assorted Paintbrushes
Disposable Plastic Plate or Paper Palette
Paper Towels
Spray Matte Varnish

*Miracle Sponge™ is a thinly compressed cellulose sponge that can be cut into desired shapes, then wet to expand. When expanded, dip in paint and use for stamping.

Painting the Container

1. Wash unfinished tin canister with vinegar, scrubbing well, then rinse thoroughly and allow to dry. This treatment removes the oils used in manufacturing tin products. If canister has been previously painted, sand well to remove all gloss and wash in vinegar as described above. When thoroughly dry, spray tin canister with metal primer. Allow to dry.

2. Paint base of canister with Crocus Yellow paint. When dry, dry brush with Antique Gold to add depth and texture. To dry brush, dip coarse brush in paint, blot several times on paper towel, then 'scrub' paint onto surface here and there.

3. Paint lid Hauser Green Light with a Lavender handle. Allow to dry.

4. Trace and transfer pansy and pot patterns on page 64 to Miracle Sponge.™ Cut out each piece with scissors or craft knife. Expand sponge in water and squeeze out as much water as possible.

5. Make a sample of stamped pansy on a piece of paper before stamping canister. This will help you determine the spacing.

6. Pour a small quantity of Tompte Red paint onto plastic plate. Rub flowerpot sponge in the red paint, thoroughly coating one side of sponge with paint. Carefully, place loaded sponge on the bottom of one side of the canister, centering flowerpot, and lightly press with fingers to transfer flowerpot shape to canister. Lift sponge straight up, being careful not to smear paint. Redip sponge and stamp flowerpot on adjacent side. Rinse sponge and save for the other two sides which will be stamped when first two sides are dry.

7. Using same technique, stamp stem and leaves using Hauser Green Light, dark part of pansy using Vintage Wine, and light part of pansy using Lavender in that order. Be careful not to smear paint already applied.

8. When dry, stamp flower center with Crocus Yellow and use a fine paintbrush to add pansy 'face' with Vintage Wine paint and leaf veins with Hauser Green Dark. Allow to dry thoroughly.

9. Repeat process for other two sides of canister. If desired, paint bottom edge of canister with Antique Gold.

10. Spray canister with matte varnish to protect the design.

Autumn Treasures

The surprising warmth and brilliant colors of autumn are reflected in this fabric interpretation of that special, fleeting time of year. A strong geometric pattern embellished with appliqués and beads makes this quilt a striking addition to your autumn home.

Autumn Treasures
Wall Quilt

Rich paprika, orange, brown, purple, and green form the backdrop for textural appliques that are quick-fused and embellished. For shine and texture, we used bouclé, silk, and brocade fabrics as well as a few cottons for the appliques. This quilt is designed to hang on the diagonal for a dramatic presentation. Prairie points and bead embellishment add to the luxuriant beauty of this quilt.

Getting Started

Refer to Accurate Seam Allowance on page 92. Whenever possible, use the Assembly Line Method on page 92. Press seams in direction of arrows. If using directional fabrics, cut all pieces so stripes are going the same direction. Blocks measure 10½" square unfinished.

Making the Blocks

1. Sew one 2" x 5" Fabric A piece and one 2" x 3" Fabric B piece together as shown. Press. Make eighteen, two of each combination.

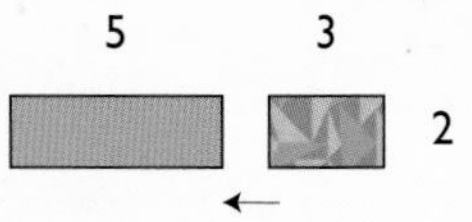

Make 18
(2 of each combination)

2. Sew one 7½" Fabric B square between two matching units from step 1 as shown, noting direction of design if using directional fabric. Press. Make nine, one of each combination.

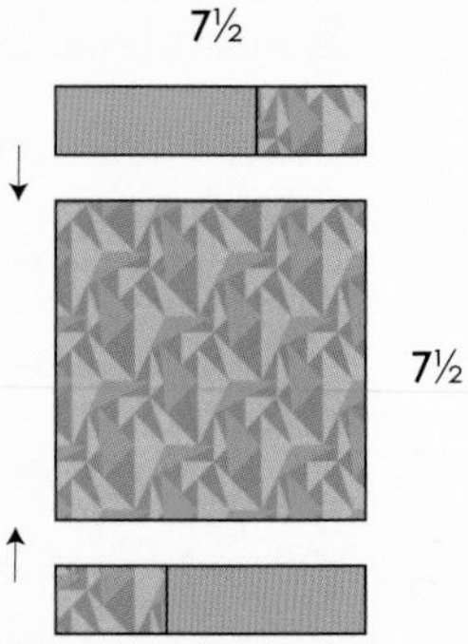

Make 9
(1 of each combination)

3. Sew one 2" x 6½" Fabric A piece and one 4½" x 2" Fabric B piece together as shown. Press. Make eighteen, two of each combination.

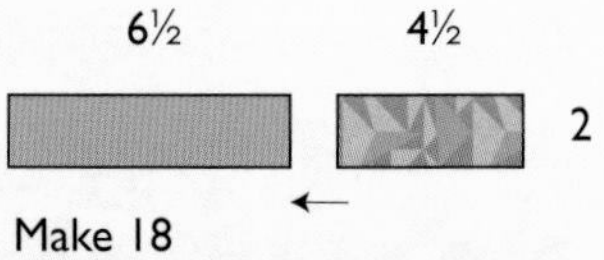

Make 18
(2 of each combination)

Autumn Treasures Wall Quilt Finished Size: 43"x 43"		FIRST CUT		SECOND CUT	
		Number of Strips or Pieces	Dimensions	Number of Pieces	Dimensions
	Fabric A Block Borders ½ yard	6	2" x 42"	18 18	2" x 6½" 2" x 5"
	Fabric B Block Center ¼ yard each of nine fabrics *Cut for each fabric	1*	7½" x 42"	1* 2* 2*	7½" square 4½" x 2"** 2" x 3"
			**For directional fabric, the measurement that is listed first runs parallel with selvage.		
BORDERS					
	First Border ⅓ yard	4	2" x 42"		
	Accent Strip ⅙ yard	4	1" x 42"		
	Prairie Points ¾ yard	5	4½" x 42"	36	4½" square
	Outside Border ¾ yard	5	5" x 42"		
	Binding ½ yard	5	2¾" x 42"		

Backing - 2 ⅝ yards
Batting - 47" x 47"
Appliqués - Assorted scraps (nine fabrics)
Lightweight Fusible Web - ¾ yard
Assorted Bead Embellishments

Fabric Requirements and Cutting Instructions

Read all instructions before beginning and use ¼"-wide seam allowances throughout. Read Cutting Strips and Pieces on page 92 prior to cutting fabrics.

4. Sew unit from step 2 between two matching units from step 3 as shown. Press. Make nine, one of each combination. Block measures 10½" square.

Make 9
(1 of each combination)
Block measures 10½" square

5. Referring to photo on page 66 and layout below, arrange and sew blocks in three rows of three blocks each. Press seams in opposite directions from row to row.

6. Sew rows together and press.

Make template of whole pattern

(Half)
Autumn Treasures
Pattern

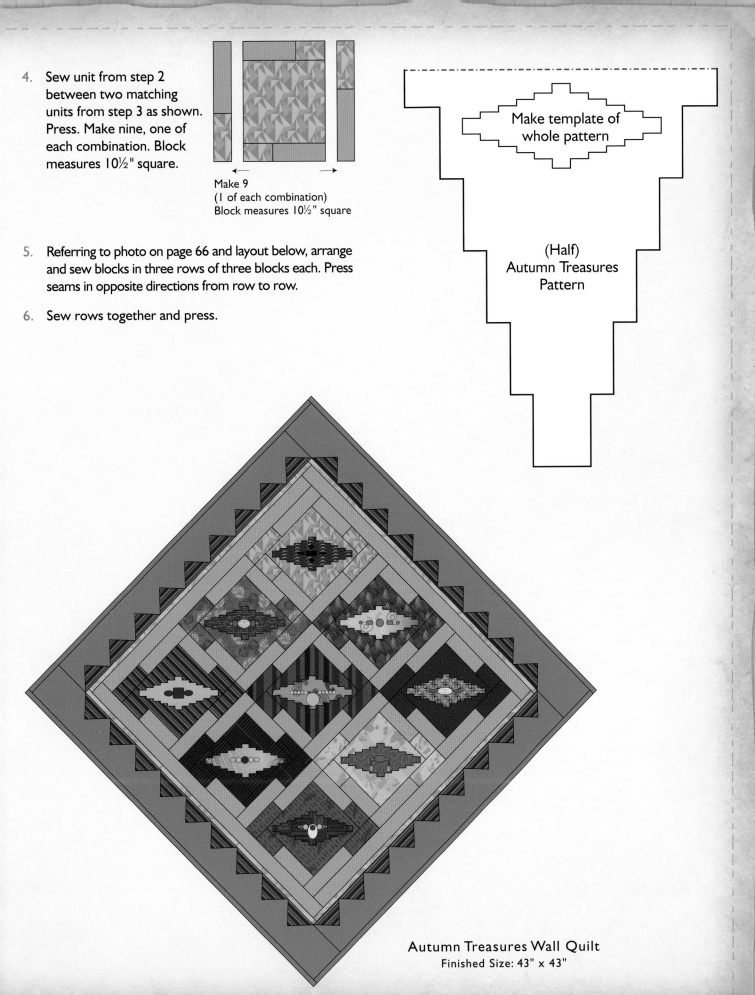

Autumn Treasures Wall Quilt
Finished Size: 43" x 43"

Adding the Appliqués

Refer to appliqué instructions on page 93. Our instructions are for Quick-Fuse Appliqué. If you prefer hand appliqué, add ¼"-wide seam allowances to patterns.

1. Refer to Quick-Fuse Appliqué on page 93. Use pattern on page 69 to trace nine appliqués on paper side of fusible web. Use brocade, silk, cotton and bouclé scraps to prepare appliqués for fusing.

2. Referring to photo on page 66 and layout on page 69, position and fuse appliqués to quilt. Finish appliqué edges with machine satin stitch or other decorative stitching as desired.

Adding the Borders

1. Referring to Adding the Borders on page 94, measure quilt through center from side to side. Trim two 2"-wide First Border strips to this measurement. Sew to top and bottom of quilt. Press seams toward border.

2. Measure quilt through center from top to bottom including borders just added. Cut two 2"-wide First Border strips to this measurement. Sew to sides of quilt. Press.

3. Fold two Accent Strips in half lengthwise, wrong sides together, and press. Measure quilt through center from side to side. Trim two Accent Strips and two Outside Border strips to this measurement. Align Accent Strip raw edges with edge of quilt and place folded edge toward center. Baste Accent Strip to top and bottom of quilt.

4. To make prairie points, fold and press one 4½" Prairie Point square in half diagonally, wrong sides together, as shown. Press. Fold and press diagonally in half again as shown to make a prairie point. Make thirty-six.

5. Refer to photo on page 66, layout on page 69, and step 6 photos. Position nine prairie points along top edge, aligning raw edges, pin and baste in place. Place Outside Border, from step 3, right sides together with prairie points. Stitch in place. Press prairie points and Accent Strip toward Outside Border. Repeat step to sew Prairie Points and Outside Border to bottom edge.

6. Measure quilt through center from top to bottom including borders just added. This measurement will be used in step 8 for Outside Border. Measure center and Accent Strips only. Cut two Accent Strips to this measurement plus 1". Fold and press Accent Strip ends under ½" to wrong side. Fold each strip in half lengthwise and press. Aligning raw edges and matching folded edges, baste to sides of quilt.

7. Arrange and pin nine prairie points to each side of quilt. Baste in place.

8. Sew Outside Border strips together end-to-end to make one continuous 5"-wide Outside Border strip. Cut two Outside Border strips to measurement from step 6. Sew border to sides of quilt. Press borders and prairie points toward Outside Border.

Layering and Finishing

1. Cut backing crosswise into two equal pieces. Sew pieces together to make one 47" x 80" (approximate) backing piece. Press and trim to 47" x 47".

2. Arrange and baste backing, batting, and top together referring to Layering the Quilt on page 94.

3. Machine or hand quilt as desired.

4. Sew 2¾"-wide binding strips end-to-end to make one continuous 2¾"-wide binding strip. Refer to Binding the Quilt on page 94 and bind quilt to finish.

Embellishing the Quilt

Adding beadwork is a fun part of making this quilt. We used a variety of beads to pull colors from one area to another, to add interest to plainer blocks, and to add dimension and shine. Refer to photo on page 66 and layout on page 69 for ideas for embellishing your quilt.

Autumn Treasures

Pillow

Colorful and textural, elegant yet easy, this exquisite pillow captures the beauty of a sunny fall day. Its elegance comes from the mixture of satins, brocades, cottons, and bouclés.

Finished Size: 20" x 20"

Materials Needed

Pillow Fabric - Thirty-six 3" squares in a variety of fabrics

Flange Fabric – ¼ yard

    Two 3" x 20½" pieces

    Two 3" x 15½" pieces

Lining – 22" Square

Backing – ½ yard

    Two 13" x 20 ½" pieces

Beads – 20 Small (optional)

Batting – 22" Square

Pillow Form Fabric - ½ yard

    Two 15½" squares

Polyester Fiberfill

Getting Started

Part of the fun of making this pillow is planning the fabric placement. Lay squares on a table or flannel board and arrange squares as desired.

Sewing together a variety of slippery and thick fabrics can be tricky. When sewing two slippery fabrics together, try basting fabrics first. A walking foot on your sewing machine also helps control movement of slippery or stretchy fabrics. Test fabrics before pressing. Decorative fabrics may need to be pressed on low heat

Fabric Requirements and Cutting Instructions

Read all instructions before beginning and use ¼"-wide seam allowances throughout. Read Cutting Strips and Pieces on page 92 prior to cutting fabrics.

Making the Pillow

1. Sew six 3" squares together to make a row. Make six rows. Press seams in opposite directions from row to row. Sew rows together to make 15 ½" square (unfinished). Press.

2. Sew 3" x 15 ½" Flange pieces to top and bottom of pillow and 3" x 20 ½" Flange pieces to sides. Press seams toward flange.

3. Refer to Finishing Pillows on page 95 step 1 to quilt top center section only. Refer to steps 2-4 to add 13" x 20 ½" backing pieces to pillow. To create Flange, sew through all layers along seam between Flange and patchwork pillow top.

4. Use metallic thread to add decorative stitching to Flange. Sew beads on as desired.

5. Refer to Pillow Forms on page 95 to make a 15" pillow form.

Rooster Banner

No garden would be complete without a friendly fowl! This rooster will brighten a dark corner of the garden or house with bold colors, textural feathers and jaunty attitude.

Rooster Banner Finished Size: 18"x 23"	FIRST CUT	
	Number of Strips or Pieces	Dimensions
Fabric A Center & Border ⅝ yard	1 1	17½" square 1½" x 17½"
Fabric B Sun ⅜ yard	1	11½" square
Fabric C Accent Stripe, Side Borders & Tabs ¼ yard	1 1 2	3" x 27" 1½" x 17½" 1" x 23½"
Fabric D Accent Stripe ⅛ yard each of four fabrics *cut for each piece	1*	1½" x 17½"

Backing - ⅝ yard
Batting - 22" x 27"
Rooster Body & Feather Appliqués - ¼ yard each of five bouclés
Hand and Feet Appliqués - Assorted scraps
Lightweight Fusible Web - ½ yard
Button for Eye

Fabric Requirements and Cutting Instructions

Read all instructions before beginning and use ¼"-wide seam allowances throughout. Read Cutting Strips and Pieces on page 92 prior to cutting fabrics.

Getting Started

Bouclé and wool appliqués provide texture and dimension to the colorful cotton background for this wallhanging. Most appliqués are fused with the exception of tail feathers which are positioned and stitched in place.

Refer to Accurate Seam Allowance on page 92. Whenever possible, use the Assembly Line Method on page 92. Press seams in direction of arrows.

Making the Wallhanging

1. Refer to Quick Corner Triangles on page 92. Making a quick corner triangle unit, sew 11½" Fabric B square to 17½" Fabric A square as shown. Press.

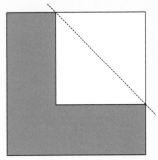

B = 11½" x 11½"
A = 17½" x 17½"

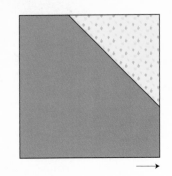

17½

2. Sew together unit from step 1, four assorted 1½" x 17½" Fabric D strips, one 1½" x 17½" Fabric A strip, and one 1½" x 17½" Fabric C strip as shown. Press.

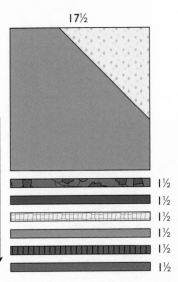

1½
1½
1½
1½
1½
1½

3. Sew unit from step 2 between two 1" x 23½" Fabric C pieces. Press.

4. Refer to photograph on page 72 and Rooster Pattern on pages 74 and 75. Cut five feathers from bouclé. The feathers are not fused, but appliquéd with a zigzag stitch sewn through the center of the feather after fusing other appliqués.

5. Refer to appliqué instructions on page 93. Our instructions are for Quick-Fuse Appliqué. If you prefer hand appliqué, add ¼"-wide seam allowances to patterns. Use patterns on pages 74 and 75 to trace remaining Rooster appliqués on lightweight fusible web. Use bouclé to prepare body and wing for fusing. Use wool or felt to prepare head, feet, beak, eye, wattle, and comb appliqués. Referring to photo, position all appliqués on wallhanging, making sure bottom edges of feathers are placed beneath rooster body. Fuse appliqués in place. Finish head, body, and wing edges with machine satin stitch or other decorative stitching as desired. Sew a zigzag or long satin stitch through center of each feather.

6. Fold 3" x 27" Fabric C piece lengthwise, right sides together. Sew along 27" length and turn right side out. Press placing seam in center of fabric piece. Cut into four 6½" lengths for hanging tabs.

7. Fold tabs in half crosswise. Referring to photo on page 72 and layout, arrange tabs on front along top edge of wallhanging. Pin or baste in place.

Layering and Finishing

1. Cut backing into 22" x 27" piece.

2. Place wallhanging top and backing right sides together and place wrong side of backing on batting piece. Using a ¼"-wide seam allowance, stitch around edges leaving a 4" opening for turning. Trim batting close to stitching and backing even with top edges. Clip corners, turn right side out, and press. Hand-stitch opening closed.

3. Machine or hand quilt as desired.

4. Referring to photo, sew button to eye of rooster.

Autumn Treasures Rooster Banner
Finished Size: 18" x 23"

Rooster Banner
Appliqué Patterns

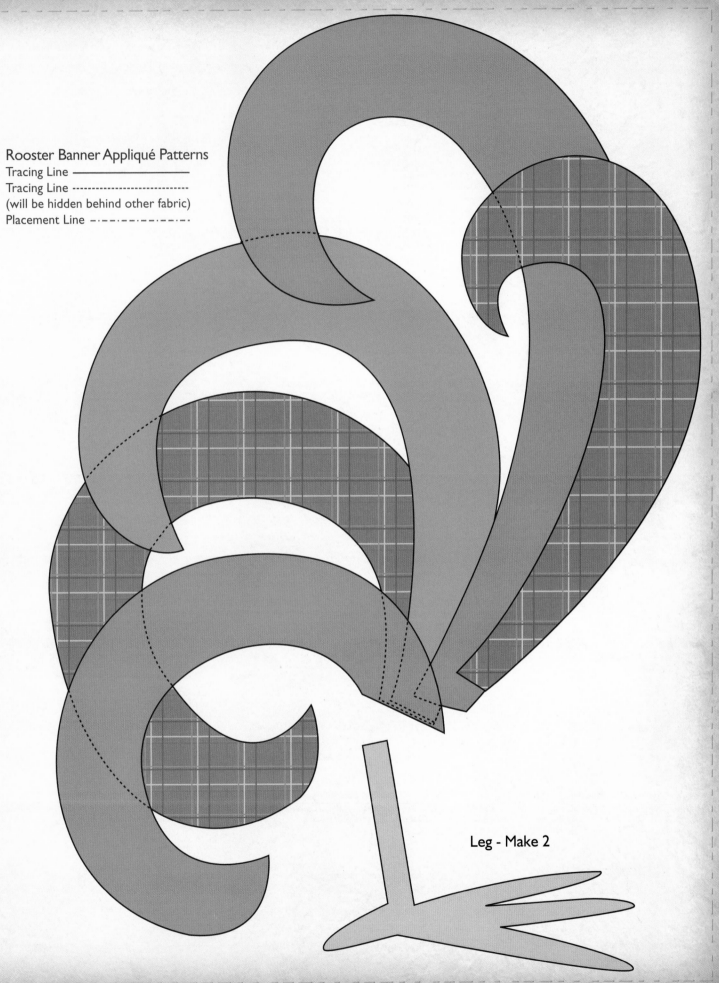

Rooster Banner Appliqué Patterns
Tracing Line ——————
Tracing Line --------------------
(will be hidden behind other fabric)
Placement Line —·—·—·—·—

Leg - Make 2

Wild Flowers

Wild, free, and untamed, beautiful blossoms grow in a profusion of color against a verdant background of patchwork. Make this lap quilt or wallhanging for a burst of brilliant color all through the year.

Wild Flowers
Lap Quilt

Wild Flowers Lap Quilt Finished Size: 46" x 66"	FIRST CUT		SECOND CUT	
	Number of Strips or Pieces	Dimensions	Number of Pieces	Dimensions
Fabric A Flower Centers ⅛ yard each of three fabrics *Cut for each fabric	1*	1½" x 42"	3* 8*	1½" x 2" 1½" x 1¼"
Fabric B Inside Petals ¼ yard each of three fabrics *Cut for each fabric	1* 1*	3¾" x 42" 1½" x 42"	3* 3* 8* 8* 11* 11*	3¾" x 1¾" 3¾" x 1½" 3" x 1½" 3" x 1¼" 1½" squares 1½" x 1¼"
Fabric C Second Row of Petals ¼ yard each of three fabrics *Cut for each fabric	1*	6" x 42"	3* 3* 3* 3*	6" x 1¾" 6" x 1½" 3¾" x 1¾" 3¾" x 1½"
Fabric D Third Row of Petals ⅓ yard each of three fabrics *Cut for each fabric	1* 1* 2*	2½" x 42" 1¾" x 42" 1½" x 42"	6* 6* 3* 6* 3*	2½" squares 2" squares 1¾" x 6" 1½" x 8¼" 1½" x 6"
Fabric E Outside Petals ⅔ yard each of three fabrics *Cut for each fabric	1* 1* 1* 1*	10½" x 42" 5½" x 42" 3¼" x 42" 2½" x 42"	6* 3* 3* 8* 8* 16* 6* 6*	10½" x 1¾" 8" x 1¾" 8" x 1½" 5½" x 1¾" 5½" x 1½" 3¼" x 1¾" 2½" squares 2" squares
Fabric F Flower Corners & Background ⅝ yard each of six fabrics *Cut for each fabric	4* 1* 1* 1*	3" x 42" 2½" x 42" 2¼" x 42" 1¾" x 42"	14* 7* 6* 16* 1* 6* 16* 16*	3" x 4½" 3" x 3½" 3" squares 3" x 2½" 3" x 1½" 2½" squares 2¼" squares 1¾" squares
Binding ⅝ yard	6	2¾" x 42"		
Backing - 3 yards Batting - 54" x 74"				

These quilt blocks are square, but a variety of strip widths and triangles give each fabric flower the informal petal arrangement of real flowers. At a glance, the flower looks perfectly symmetrical, but close observation reveals that it is slightly askew which adds visual interest to the quilt.

Fabric Requirements and Cutting Instructions

Read all instructions before beginning and use ¼"-wide seam allowances throughout. Read Cutting Strips and Pieces on page 92 prior to cutting fabrics.

Getting Started

Large Flower blocks are 10½" square (unfinished) and Small Flowers are 5½" square (unfinished). The background is pieced to form 5½" x 10½" (unfinished) units. When cutting fabric, we recommend that all strips be placed in labeled re-closable plastic bags to make sure that the correct fabric width and length is added when instructed.

Refer to Accurate Seam Allowance on page 92. Whenever possible, use the Assembly Line Method on page 92. Press seams in direction of arrows.

Making Large Flower Block

You will be making nine large blocks, three each of pink, red, and orange in the following steps.

1. Sew 1½" x 2" Fabric A piece between one 1½" Fabric B square and one 1½" x 1¼" Fabric B piece as shown. Press. Make nine, three of each combination.

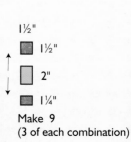

1½"
1½"
2"
1¼"

Make 9
(3 of each combination)

2. Sew unit from step 1 between one 3¾" x 1½" Fabric B piece and one 3¾" x 1¾" Fabric B piece as shown. Press. Make nine, three of each combination.

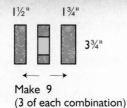

1½" 1¾" 3¾"

Make 9
(3 of each combination)

3. Sew unit from step 2, between one 3¾" x 1¾" Fabric C piece and one 3¾" x 1½" Fabric C piece as shown. Press. Make nine, three of each combination.

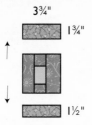

3¾"

1¾"

1½"

Make 9
(3 of each combination)

4. Sew unit from step 3 between one 6" x 1¾" Fabric C piece and one 6" x 1½" Fabric C piece as shown. Press. Make nine, three of each combination.

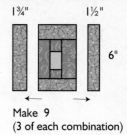

1¾" 1½"

6"

Make 9
(3 of each combination)

5. Refer to Quick Corner Triangles on page 92. Making quick corner triangle units, sew two 2" Fabric D squares to unit from step 4 as shown. Press. Making quick corner triangles sew two 2½" Fabric D squares to unit as shown. Press. Make nine, three of each combination.

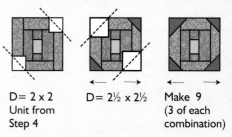

D= 2 x 2
Unit from
Step 4

D= 2½ x 2½

Make 9
(3 of each combination)

6. Sew unit from step 5 between one 1½" x 6" Fabric D piece and one 1¾" x 6" Fabric D piece as shown. Press. Make nine, three of each combination.

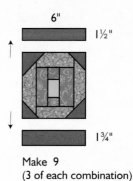

6"

1½"

1¾"

Make 9
(3 of each combination)

7. Sew unit from step 6 between two 1½" x 8¼" Fabric D pieces as shown. Press. Make nine, three of each combination.

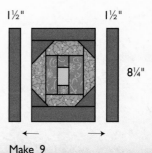

1½" 1½"

8¼"

Make 9
(3 of each combination)

Wild Flowers Lap Quilt
Finished Size: 46" x 66"

8. Making quick corner triangle units, sew two 2" Fabric E squares to unit from step 7 as shown. Press. Making quick corner triangle units, sew two 2½" Fabric E squares to unit as shown. Press. Make nine, three of each combination.

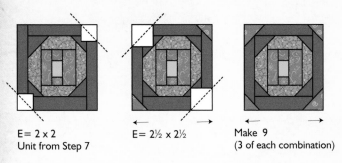

E= 2 x 2
Unit from Step 7

E= 2½ x 2½

Make 9
(3 of each combination)

9. Sew unit from step 8 between one 8" x 1½" Fabric E piece and one 8" x 1¾" Fabric E piece as shown. Press. Make nine, three of each combination.

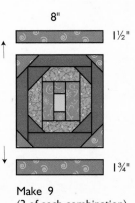

8"

1½"

1¾"

Make 9
(3 of each combination)

10. Sew unit from step 9 between two 10½" x 1¾" Fabric E pieces as shown. Press. Make nine, three of each combination.

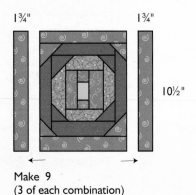

1¾"   1¾"

10½"

Make 9
(3 of each combination)

11. Making quick corner triangle units sew two matching 3" Fabric F squares and two matching 2½" Fabric F squares to unit from step 10. Press. Make nine, three of each combination. Block measures 10½" square. Note: Three different greens were used, one shade for pink blocks, one for red, and a different one for orange blocks.

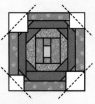

F= 3 x 3
F= 2½ x 2½
Unit from Step 10

Make 3
Block measures 10½" square

Red Flower
Make 3
Block measures
10½" square

Orange Flower
Make 3
Block measures
10½" square

Making the Small Flower Block

1. Sew one 1½" x 1¼" Fabric A piece between one 1½" Fabric B square and one 1½" x 1¼" Fabric B piece as shown. Press. Make twenty-two, seven pink, seven red, and eight orange units.

1½"

1½"
1¼"
1¼"

Make 22
(7 pink, 7 red, 8 orange)

2. Sew unit from step 1 between one 3" x 1½" Fabric B piece and one 3" x 1¼" Fabric B piece as shown. Press. Make twenty-two, seven pink, seven red, and eight orange units.

1½"   1¼"

3"

Make 22
(7 pink, 7 red, 8 orange)

3. Sew unit from step 2 between two 3¼" x 1¾" Fabric E pieces as shown. Press. Make twenty-two, seven pink, seven red, and eight orange units.

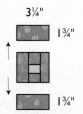

3¼"

1¾"

1¾"

Make 22
(7 pink, 7 red, 8 orange)

4. Sew unit from step 3 between one 5½" x 1½" Fabric E piece and one 5½" x 1¾" Fabric E piece as shown. Press. Make twenty-two, seven pink, seven red, and eight orange units.

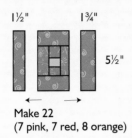

Make 22
(7 pink, 7 red, 8 orange)

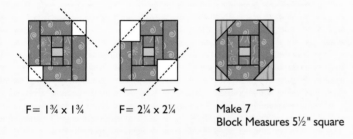

Make 7   Make 7   Make 8

5. Making quick corner triangle units, sew two matching 1¾" Fabric F squares to one unit from step 4 as shown. Press. Making quick corner triangle units, sew two matching 2¼" Fabric F squares to unit as shown. Press. Make twenty-two, seven pink, seven red, and eight orange units. Block measures 5½" square.

F = 1¾ x 1¾   F = 2¼ x 2¼   Make 7
                                 Block Measures 5½" square

Make 7   Make 8
Block   Block
Measures   Measures
5½" square   5½" square

Making the Background

1. To make Unit 1, sew two 3" x 4½" and one 3" x 2½" Fabric F pieces together as shown to make a 3" x 10½" unit. Referring to photo on page 76 and layout on page 79, sew assorted combinations and arrangements. Make nineteen units.

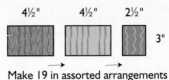

4½"   4½"   2½"

                                3"

Make 19 in assorted arrangements

2. To make Unit 2, sew two 3" x 3½" and two 3" x 2½" Fabric F pieces together to make a 3" x 10½" unit as shown. Press. Referring to photo on page 76 and layout on page 79, sew assorted combinations and arrangements. Make nineteen units .

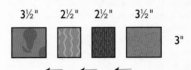

3½"   2½"   2½"   3½"

                                3"

Make 19 in assorted arrangements

3. Sew Units 1 and 2 together in pairs making sure seams and like color fabrics are off-set from each other as shown. Press. Make sixteen units. Unit measures 5½" x 10½".

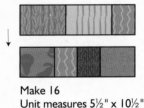

Make 16
Unit measures 5½" x 10½"

4. For variety, one 3" x 1½" Fabric F piece was sewn to Unit 1 to add interest and break the pattern. Make three. Arrange and sew this unit to one Unit 2 off-setting seams and colors. Make three units and trim to 5½" x 10½".

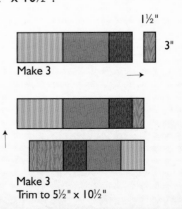

1½"

                                3"

Make 3

Make 3
Trim to 5½" x 10½"

Assembly

1. Refering to diagram below, (dotted lines), arrange and sew 5½" x 10½" background units and flower blocks as shown. Press.

2. Sew large units (areas within red lines) together and press.

Adding the Border

Refer to photo on page 76 and layout on page 79.

1. Arrange and sew together assorted 3" x 4½" and 3" x 2½" Fabric F pieces to make two 3" x 40½" border rows. Sew these rows to top and bottom of quilt. Press seams toward border.

2. Arrange and sew together assorted 3" x 4½" and 3" x 2½" Fabric F pieces to make two 3" x 65½" border rows. Sew these rows to sides of quilt. Press seams toward border.

Layering and Finishing

1. Cut backing crosswise into two equal pieces. Sew pieces together to make one 54" x 80" (approximate) backing piece. Press.

2. Arrange and baste backing, batting, and top together referring to Layering the Quilt on page 94.

3. Machine or hand quilt as desired.

4. Sew 2¾"-wide binding strips together end-to-end to make one continuous 2¾"-wide binding strip. Refer to Binding the Quilt on page 94 and bind quilt to finish.

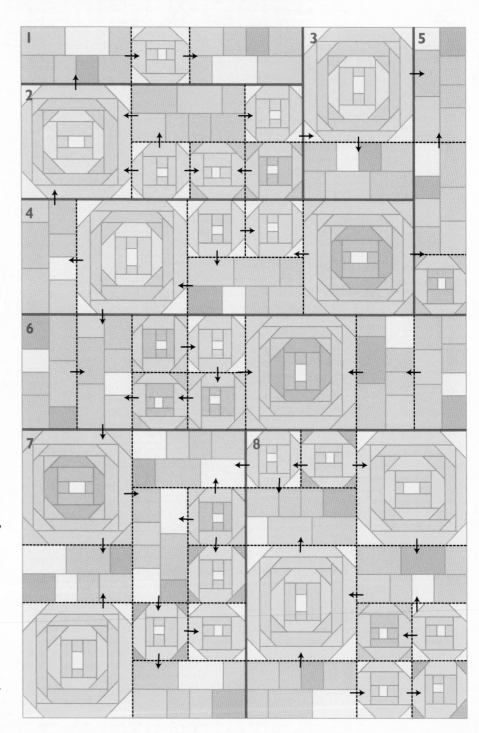

Wild Flowers

Wallhanging

Wild Flowers Wallhanging Finished Size: 31" x 31"	FIRST CUT	
	Number of Strips or Pieces	Dimensions
Fabric A Flower Centers Four Assorted Scraps *Cut for each fabric	1*	1½" x 2"
Fabric B Inside Petals Four Assorted Scraps *Cut for each fabric	1* 1* 1* 1*	1¾" x 3¾" 1½" x 3¾" 1½" square 1½" x 1¼"
Fabric C Second Row of Petals ⅛ yard each of four fabrics *Cut for each fabric	1* 1* 1* 1*	1¾" x 6" 1¾" x 3¾" 1½" x 6 1½" x 3¾"
Fabric D Third Row of Petals ⅛ yard each of four fabrics *Cut for each fabric	2* 2* 1* 2* 1*	2½" squares 2" squares 1¾" x 6" 1½" x 8¼" 1½" x 6"
Fabric E Outside Petals ⅛ yard each of four fabrics *Cut for each fabric	2* 2* 2* 1* 1*	2½" squares 2" squares 1¾" x 10½" 1¾" x 8" 1½" x 8"
Fabric F Block Corners ⅛ yard each of four fabrics	2* 2*	3" squares 2½" squares
BORDERS		
Border ⅛ yard each of six fabrics		
Border Foundation ⅞ yard	2 2	6½" x 32" 6½" x 23"
Binding ⅜ yards	4	2¾" x 42"
Backing - 1 yard Batting - 35" x 35"		

Lop-sided blossoms form the center of this wall quilt. Crazy patch borders surround the flowers to make a garden patch for your wall.

Fabric Requirements and Cutting Instructions

Read all instructions before beginning and use ¼"-wide seam allowances throughout. Read Cutting Strips and Pieces on page 92 prior to cutting fabrics.

Getting Started

Flower blocks are 10½" square (unfinished). Scraps may be used for the foundation crazy patch border or use ⅛ yard strips to cut patches.

Refer to Accurate Seam Allowance on page 92. Whenever possible, use the Assembly Line Method on page 92. Press seams in direction of arrows.

Making the Blocks

1. Sew 1½" x 2" Fabric A piece between one 1½" Fabric B square and one 1½" x 1¼" Fabric B piece as shown. Press. Make four, one of each color combination.

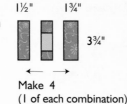

1½"

1½" — 1½"

2"

1¼"

Make 4
(1 of each combination)

2. Sew unit from step 1 between one 1½" x 3¾" Fabric B piece and one 1¾" x 3¾" Fabric B piece as shown. Press. Make four, one of each color combination.

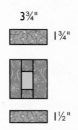

1½"   1¾"

3¾"

Make 4
(1 of each combination)

3. Sew unit from step 2 between one 1¾" x 3¾" Fabric C piece and one 1½" x 3¾" Fabric C piece as shown. Press. Make four, one of each color combination.

3¾"

1¾"

1½"

Make 4
(1 of each combination)

4. Sew unit from step 3 between one 1¾" x 6" Fabric C piece and one 1½" x 6" Fabric C piece as shown. Press. Make four, one of each color combination.

1¾"   1½"

6"

Make 4
(1 of each combination)

5. Refer to Quick Corner Triangles on page 92. Making quick corner triangle units, sew two 2" Fabric D squares to unit from step 5 as shown. Press. Making quick corner triangle units sew two 2½" Fabric D squares to unit as shown. Press. Make four, one of each color combination.

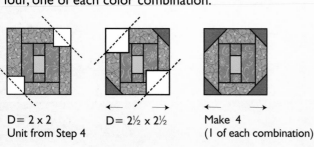

D= 2 x 2
Unit from Step 4

D= 2½ x 2½

Make 4
(1 of each combination)

6. Sew unit from step 5 between one 1½" x 6" Fabric D piece and one 1¾" x 6" Fabric D piece as shown. Press. Make four, one of each color combination.

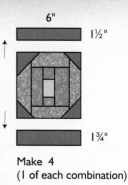

6"

1½"

1¾"

Make 4
(1 of each combination)

7. Sew unit from step 6 between two 1½" x 8¼" Fabric D pieces as shown. Press. Make four, one of each color combination.

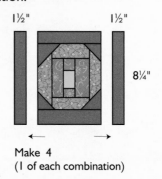

1½"   1½"

8¼"

Make 4
(1 of each combination)

8. Making quick corner triangle units, sew two 2" Fabric E squares to unit from step 7 as shown. Press. Making quick corner triangle units, sew two 2½" Fabric E squares to unit as shown. Press. Make four, one of each color combination.

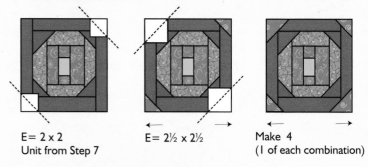

E= 2 x 2
Unit from Step 7

E= 2½ x 2½

Make 4
(1 of each combination)

9. Sew unit from step 8 between one 1½" x 8" Fabric E piece and one 1¾" x 8" Fabric E piece as shown. Press. Make four, one of each color combination.

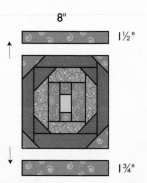

8"

1½"

1¾"

Make 4
(1 of each combination)

10. Sew unit from step 9 between two 1¾" x 10½" Fabric E pieces as shown. Press. Make four, one of each color combination.

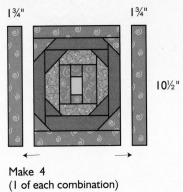

1¾"   1¾"

10½"

Make 4
(1 of each combination)

11. Making quick corner triangle units sew two 2½" and two 3" Fabric F squares to corners of unit from step 10. Press. Make four, paying attention to direction of block and placement of squares, make one of each color combination. Block measures 10½" square.

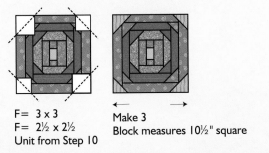

F = 3 x 3
F = 2½ x 2½
Unit from Step 10

Make 3
Block measures 10½" square

12. Referring to photo on page 83 and layout, arrange and sew blocks in pairs. Press. Sew pairs together. Press.

Wild Flowers Wallhanging
Finished Size: 31" x 31"

Making the Borders

1. To make a crazy patch border use an assortment of green squares, rectangles, triangles, and other shapes. Sew assorted fabric pieces to 6½" x 22½" foundation piece, matching right sides together and pressing after each fabric addition. Trim as needed being careful not to cut foundation. Be sure to cover all edges of foundation. Press and trim to 5½" x 20½". Make two.

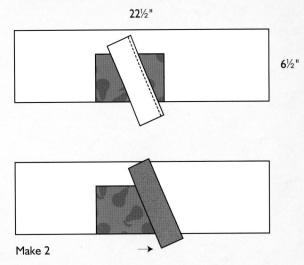

22½"

6½"

Make 2

2. Repeating step 1 sew green fabric pieces to two 6½" x 32" foundation pieces. Press and trim to 5½" x 30½".

3. Sew 5½" x 20½" border units to top and bottom of quilt. Press seams toward border.

4. Sew 5½" x 30½" border units to sides of quilt. Press.

Layering and Finishing

1. Trim backing to 36" x 36". Arrange and baste backing, batting, and top together referring to Layering the Quilt on page 94.

2. Machine or hand quilt as desired.

3. Refer to Binding the Quilt on page 94 and bind quilt to finish.

Sweet Pea

A profusion of bright colors makes a riotous revelry of pattern and hue on this entrancing bed quilt. When you look at it carefully, light and dark stars orbit in the quilt bringing subtle order to the bounty of beautiful colors.

Sweet Pea
Bed Quilt

Sweet Pea Bed Quilt Finished Size: 71"x 86½"	FIRST CUT		SECOND CUT	
	Number of Strips or Pieces	Dimensions	Number of Pieces	Dimensions
Fabric A Light Fabrics ⅝ yard each of ten fabrics for each color *Cut for each fabric	1*	6½" x 42"	2*	6½" squares (cut in half diagonally)
	2*	3½" x 42"	8	3½" x 5½"
			8	3½" squares
	2*	3" x 42"	16	3" squares
Fabric B Dark Fabrics ¾ yard each of ten fabrics for each color *Cut for each fabric	1*	6½" x 42"	3*	6½" squares (cut in half diagonally)
	3*	3½" x 42"	8	3½" x 5½"
			10	3½" squares
	2*	3" x 42"	16	3" squares
BORDERS				
First Border ½ yard	8	1½" x 42"		
Second Border ⅞ yard	8	3½" x 42"		
Binding ⅔ yard	8	2¾" x 42"		
Backing - 5⅓ yards Batting - 79" x 96"				

Fabric Requirements and Cutting Instructions

Read all instructions before beginning and use ¼"-wide seam allowances throughout. Read Cutting Strips and Pieces on page 92 prior to cutting fabrics.

TIP TWISTING SEAMS

For ease in construction when using quarter-square triangles we add a twist…

When pressing the last seam, twist the center of the seam so that it fans into a square. The stitches in the "square" will pull loose. All seam allowances fan out in the same direction to eliminate excess bulk.

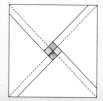

Getting Started

Star Blocks are made with bright summer colors and set on point. Side setting triangles and corner units are made with a portion of the same design. Light star points are centered and surrounded by dark fabrics, and dark star points are centered and surrounded by light fabrics. Blocks measure 11½" square unfinished.

Refer to Accurate Seam Allowance on page 92. Whenever possible, use the Assembly Line Method on page 92. Press seams in direction of arrows.

Making the Blocks

1. Sew two Fabric A triangles together as shown to make half-square triangles. Press seam to one side. Make twenty. Sew two Fabric B triangles together to make half-square triangles. Press. Make twenty-six.

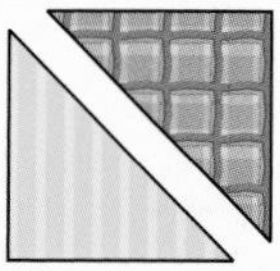

Make 46
20 Fabric A
26 Fabric B

2. Make a quarter-square triangle unit by drawing a diagonal line on wrong side of one Fabric A unit from step 1 in opposite direction from seam as shown. Place marked unit right sides together with a contrasting Fabric A unit from step 1. Sew a scant ¼" away from drawn line on both sides, as shown. Cut on drawn line. Press seams so they all rotate in the same direction, twisting center intersection (see TIP). Square each unit to 5½". Make twenty Fabric A quarter-square triangle units and label Unit 1. Sew six Fabric B half-square triangle units from step 1 to make twelve Fabric B quarter-square triangle units, square to 5½" and label Unit 2. Remaining Fabric B half-square triangles will be used in the side setting triangles.

  Unit 1 Unit 2

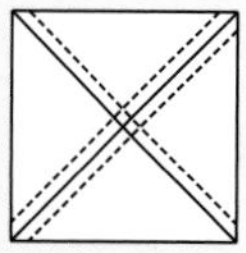

Make 16
10 Fabric A
6 Fabric B

Make 20
Square to 5½"

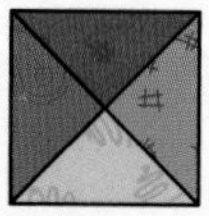

Make 12
Square to 5½"

3. Refer to Quick Corner Triangles on page 92. Making quick corner triangle units, sew two matching 3" Fabric B squares to one 3½" x 5½" Fabric A piece as shown to make Unit 3. Press. Make eighty (twenty sets of four with matching triangles). Making quick corner triangle units, sew two matching 3" Fabric A squares to one 3½" x 5½" Fabric B piece as shown to make Unit 4. Press. Make eighty (twelve sets of four with matching star points and seven sets of two with matching triangles).

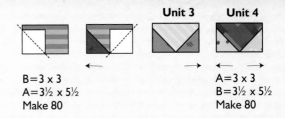

Unit 3

B=3 x 3
A=3½ x 5½
Make 80

Unit 4

A=3 x 3
B=3½ x 5½
Make 80

Sweet Pea Bed Quilt
Finished Size: 71" x 86½"

4. Sew one of Unit 3 between two contrasting 3½" Fabric A squares as shown. Press. Make forty. Sew one of Unit 4 between two contrasting 3½" Fabric B squares as shown. Press. Make forty-two.

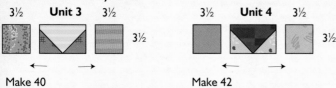

Make 40   Make 42

5. Sew one Unit 1 from step 2 between two of Unit 3 from step 3 as shown matching triangles. Press. Make twenty. Sew one Unit 2 from step 2 between two of Unit 4 from step 3 as shown. Press. Make twelve.

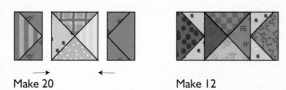

Make 20   Make 12

6. Sew one Unit 1 from step 5 between two of Unit 3 from step 4 matching triangles as shown to make Block One. Press. Make twenty. Sew one Unit 2 from step 5 between two of Unit 4 from step 4 to make Block Two. Press. Make twelve. Blocks measure 11½" square.

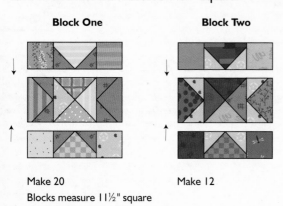

Block One   **Block Two**

Make 20   Make 12

Blocks measure 11½" square

7. To make Side Setting Triangles, sew one 3½" Fabric B square to one Unit 4 from step 3. Press. Sew this unit to one Fabric B half-square triangle from step 1. Press. Make fourteen.

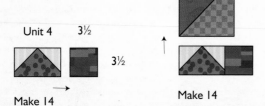

Unit 4   3½"

Make 14   Make 14

Side Setting Triangles

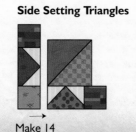

Make 14

8. Sew one Unit 4 from step 4 to unit from step 7 as shown, matching triangles. Press. Make fourteen and label Side Setting Triangles.

9. To make Corner Setting Triangles, sew one Unit 4 from step 4 to one Fabric B triangle. Press and label. Make four.

Corner Setting Triangle

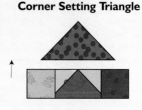

Make 4

Assembly

1. Sew one Corner Setting Triangle to Block One. Press. Sew this unit between two side setting triangles as shown. Press. Make two. These will be the first and last rows of the quilt top (rows 1 and 8).

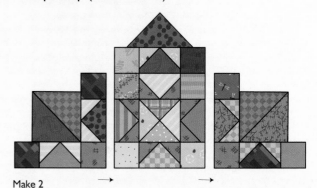

Make 2

2. Referring to Assembly Layout, arrange and sew two Side Setting Triangles, two of Block One, and one of Block Two to make rows 2 and 7. Press seams opposite from rows in step 1.

3. Referring to Assembly Layout, arrange and sew two Side Setting Triangles, three of Block One, and two of Block Two to make rows 3 and 6. Press seams opposite from rows in step 2.

4. Referring to Assembly Layout, arrange and sew one Side Setting Triangles, four of Block One, three of Block Two and one Corner Setting Triangle to make rows 4 and 5. Press seams opposite from rows in step 3.

5. Referring to Assembly Layout, arrange and sew rows 1 through 8 together. Press. Using a temporary marker and straight edge, draw a straight line from corner to corner on all four sides.

Adding the Borders

1. Refer to Adding the Borders on page 94. Sew 1½" x 42" First Border strips together end-to-end to make one continuous 1½"-wide First Border strip. Press. Measure quilt from line to line through center from side to side. Cut two 1½"-wide border strips to this measurement. Sew to top and bottom of quilt along drawn line. Trim Side Setting Triangles leaving ¼" seam allowance. Press seams toward border.

2. Measure quilt through center from top to bottom including borders just added. Cut two 1½"-wide First Border strips to this measurement. Sew to sides of quilt. Trim Side Setting Triangles leaving ¼" seam allowance. Press.

3. Refer to steps 1 and 2 to join, measure, trim, and sew 3½"-wide Outside Border strips to top, bottom, and sides of quilt. Press.

Layering and Finishing

1. Cut backing crosswise into two equal pieces. Sew pieces together to make one 80" x 96"(approximate) backing piece. Press.

2. Arrange and baste backing, batting, and top together referring to Layering the Quilt on page 94.

3. Machine or hand quilt as desired.

4. Sew 2¾"-wide binding strips end-to-end to make one continuous 2¾"-wide binding strip. Refer to Binding the Quilt on page 94 and bind quilt to finish.

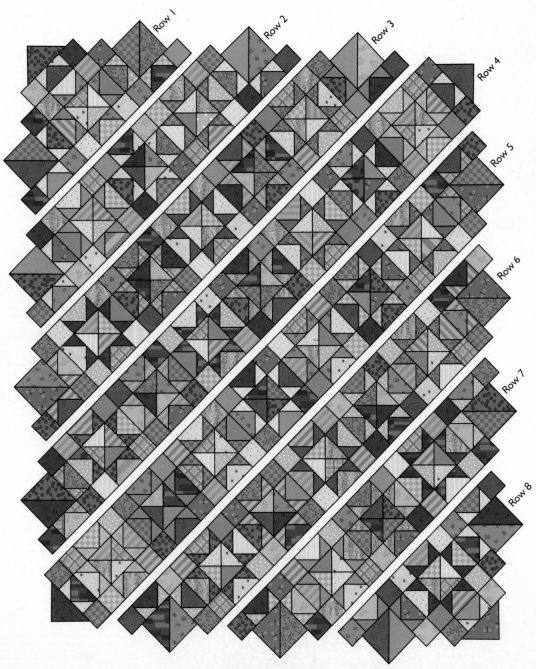

Assembly Layout

General Directions

Cutting Strips & Pieces

We recommend washing cotton fabrics in cold water and pressing before making projects in this book. Using a rotary cutter, see-through ruler, and a cutting mat, cut the strips and pieces for the project. If indicated on the Cutting Chart, some will need to be cut again into smaller strips and pieces. Make second cuts in order shown to maximize use of fabric. The yardage amounts and cutting instructiions are based on an approximate fabric width of 42".

Fussy Cut

To make a "fussy cut," carefully position ruler or template over a selected design in fabric. Include seam allowances before cutting desired pieces.

Assembly Line Method

Whenever possible, use an assembly line method. Position pieces right sides together and line up next to sewing machine. Stitch first unit together, then continue sewing others without breaking threads. When all units are sewn, clip threads to separate. Press seams in the direction of arrows.

Accurate Seam Allowance

Accurate seam allowances are always important, but especially when the blocks contain many pieces and the quilt top contains multiple pieced borders. If each seam is off as little as $\frac{1}{16}$", you'll soon find yourself struggling with components that just won't fit.

To ensure seams are a perfect $\frac{1}{4}$"-wide, try this simple test: Cut three strips of fabric, each exactly $1\frac{1}{2}$" x 12". With right sides together, and long raw edges aligned, sew two strips together, carefully maintaining a $\frac{1}{4}$" seam. Press seam to one side. Add the third strip to complete the strip set. Press and measure. The finished strip set should measure $3\frac{1}{2}$" x 12". The center strip should measure 1"-wide, the two outside strips $1\frac{1}{4}$"-wide, and the seam allowances exactly $\frac{1}{4}$".

If your measurements differ, check to make sure that seams have been pressed flat. If strip set still doesn't "measure up," try stitching a new strip set, adjusting the seam allowance until a perfect $\frac{1}{4}$"-wide seam is achieved.

Pressing

Pressing is very important for accurate seam allowances. Press seams using either steam or dry heat with an "up and down" motion. Do not use side-to-side motion as this will distort the unit or block. Set the seam by pressing along the line of stitching, then press seams to one side as indicated by project instructions. Press seams in the direction of arrows on diagrams.

Quick Corner Triangles

Quick corner triangles are formed by simply sewing fabric squares to other squares or rectangles. The directions and diagrams with each project illustrate what size pieces to use and where to place squares on the corresponding piece. Follow steps 1–3 below to make quick corner triangle units.

1. With pencil and ruler, draw diagonal line on wrong side of fabric square that will form the triangle. This will be your sewing line.

Sewing line

2. With right sides together, place square on corresponding piece. Matching raw edges, pin in place, and sew ON drawn line. Trim off excess fabric, leaving $\frac{1}{4}$"-wide seam allowance as shown.

Trim $\frac{1}{4}$"away
from sewing line

3. Press seam in direction of arrow as shown in step-by-step project diagram. Measure completed quick corner triangle unit to ensure the greatest accuracy.

Finished
quick corner
triangle unit

Quick-Fuse Appliqué

Quick-fuse appliqué is a method of adhering appliqué pieces to a background with fusible web. For quick and easy results, simply quick-fuse appliqué pieces in place. Use sewable, lightweight fusible web for the projects in this book unless otherwise indicated. Finish raw edges with stitching as desired. Laundering is not recommended unless edges are finished.

1. With paper side up, lay fusible web over appliqué pattern. Leaving ½" space between pieces, trace all elements of design. Cut around traced pieces, approximately ¼" outside traced line.

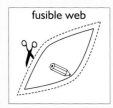

fusible web

2. With paper side up, position and press fusible web to wrong side of selected fabrics. Follow manufacturer's directions for iron temperature and fusing time. Cut out each piece on traced line.

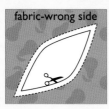

fabric-wrong side

3. Remove paper backing from pieces. A thin film will remain on wrong side of fabric. Position and fuse all pieces of one appliqué design at a time onto background, referring to photos for placement. Fused design will be the reverse of traced pattern.

Appliqué Pressing Sheet

An appliqué pressing sheet is very helpful when there are many small elements to apply using a quick-fuse appliqué technique. The pressing sheet allows small items to be bonded together before applying them to the background. The sheet is coated with a special material that prevents fusible web from adhering permanently to the sheet. Follow manufacturer's directions. Remember to let fabric cool completely before lifting it from the appliqué sheet. If not cooled, the fusible web could remain on the sheet instead of on the fabric.

Machine Appliqué

This technique should be used when you are planning to launder quick-fuse projects. Several different stitches can be used: small narrow zigzag stitch, satin stitch, blanket stitch, or another decorative machine stitch. Use an open toe appliqué foot if your machine has one. Use a stabilizer to obtain even stitches and help prevent puckering. Always practice first to check machine settings.

1. Fuse all pieces following Quick-Fuse Appliqué directions.

2. Cut a piece of stabilizer large enough to extend beyond the area to be stitched. Pin to the wrong side of fabric.

3. Select thread to match appliqué.

4. Following the order that appliqués were positioned, stitch along the edges of each section. Anchor beginning and ending stitches by tying off or stitching in place two or three times.

5. Complete all stitching, then remove stabilizer.

Hand Appliqué

Hand appliqué is easy when you start out with the right supplies. Cotton and machine embroidery thread are easy to work with. Pick a color that matches the appliqué fabric as closely as possible. Use appliqué or silk pins for holding shapes in place and a long, thin needle, such as a sharp, for stitching.

1. Make a template for every shape in the appliqué design. Use a dotted line to show where pieces overlap.

2. Place template on right side of appliqué fabric. Trace around template.

3. Cut out shapes ¼" beyond traced line.

4. Position shapes on background fabric, referring to quilt layout. Pin shapes in place.

5. When layering and stitching appliqué shapes, always work from background to foreground. Where shapes overlap, do not turn under and stitch edges of bottom pieces. Turn and stitch the edges of the piece on top.

6. Use the traced line as your turn-under guide. Entering from the wrong side of the appliqué shape, bring the needle up on the traced line. Using the tip of the needle, turn under the fabric along the traced line. Using blind stitch, stitch along the folded edge to join the appliqué shape to the background fabric. Turn under and stitch about ¼" at a time.

Adding the Borders

1. Measure quilt through the center from side to side. Trim two border strips to this measurement. Sew to top and bottom of quilt. Press seams toward border

2. Measure quilt through the center from top to bottom, including borders added in step 1. Trim border strips to this measurement. Sew to sides and press. Repeat to add additional borders.

Mitered Borders

A mitered border is usually "fussy cut" to highlight a motif or design. Borders are cut slightly longer than needed to allow for centering of motif or matching corners.

1. Cut the border strips or strip sets as indicated for quilt.

2. Measure each side of the quilt and mark center with a pin. Fold each border strip in half crosswise to find its midpoint and mark with a pin. Using the side measurements, measure out from the midpoint and place a pin to show where the edges of the quilt will be.

midpoint

3. Align a border strip to quilt. Pin at midpoints and pin-marked ends first, then along entire side, easing to fit if necessary.

4. Sew border to quilt, stopping and starting ¼" from pin-marked end points. Repeat to sew all four border strips to quilt.

quilt front

5. Fold corner of quilt diagonally, right sides together, matching seams and borders. Place a long ruler along fold line extending across border. Draw a diagonal line across border from fold to edge of border. This is the stitching line. Starting at ¼" mark, stitch on drawn line. Check for squareness, then trim excess. Press seam open.

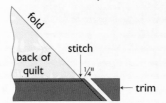

Layering the Quilt

1. Cut backing and batting 4" to 8" larger than quilt top.

2. Lay pressed backing on bottom (right side down), batting in middle, and pressed quilt top (right side up) on top. Make sure everything is centered and that backing and batting are flat. Backing and batting will extend beyond quilt top.

3. Begin basting in center and work toward outside edges. Baste vertically and horizontally, forming a 3"–4" grid. Baste or pin completely around edge of quilt top. Quilt as desired. Remove basting.

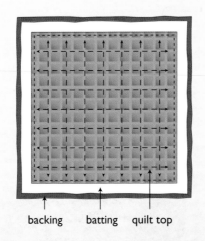

backing   batting   quilt top

Binding the Quilt

1. Trim batting and backing to ¼" beyond raw edge of quilt top. This will add fullness to binding.

2. Join binding strips to make one continuous strip if needed. To join, place strips perpendicular to each other, right sides together, matching diagonal cut edges and allowing tips of angles to extend approximately ¼" beyond edges. Sew ¼"-wide seams. Continue stitching ends together to make the desired length. Press seams open.

3. Fold and press binding strips in half lengthwise with wrong sides together.

4. Measure quilt through center from side to side. Cut two binding strips to this measurement. Lay binding strips on top and bottom edges of quilt top with raw edges of binding and quilt top aligned. Sew through all layers, ¼" from quilt edge. Press

Front of Quilt

binding away from quilt top.

5. Measure quilt through center from top to bottom, including binding just added. Cut two binding strips to this measurement and sew to sides through all layers, including binding just added. Press.

6. Folding top and bottom first, fold binding around to back then repeat with sides. Press and pin in position. Hand-stitch binding in place using a blind stitch.

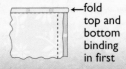

←fold top and bottom binding in first

Finishing Pillows

1. Layer batting between pillow top and lining. Baste. Hand or machine quilt as desired, unless otherwise indicated. Trim batting and lining even with raw edge of pillow top.

2. Narrow hem one long edge of each backing piece by folding under ¼" to wrong side. Press. Fold under ¼" again to wrong side. Press. Stitch along folded edge.

3. With right sides up, lay one backing piece over second piece so hemmed edges overlap, making backing unit the same measurement as the pillow top. Baste backing pieces together at top and bottom where they overlap.

4. With right sides together, position and pin pillow top to backing. Using ¼"-wide seam, sew around edges, trim corners, turn right side out, and press.

Pillow Forms

Cut two pieces of fabric to finished size of pillow form plus ½". Place right sides together, aligning raw edges. Using ¼"-wide seam, sew around all edges, leaving 4" opening for turning. Trim corners and turn right side out. Stuff to desired fullness with polyester fiberfill and hand-stitch opening closed.

General Painting Directions

Read all instructions on paint products before using and carefully follow manufacturer's instructions and warnings. For best results, allow paint to dry thoroughly between each coat and between processes unless directed otherwise. Wear face mask and safety goggles when sanding. Rubber gloves are recommended when handling stains and other finishing products.

Couching Technique

Couching is a method of attaching a textured yarn, cord, or fiber to fabric for decorative purposes. Use an open-toe embroidery foot, couching foot, or a zigzag presser foot and matching or monofilament thread. Sew with a long zigzag stitch just barely wider than the cord or yarn. Stabilizer on the wrong side of fabric is recommended. Place the yarn, cord, or fiber on right side of fabric and zigzag to attach as shown. A hand-stitch can be used if desired.

Couching

Embroidery Stitch Guide

Stem Stitch

Satin Stitch

French Knot

Blanket Stitch

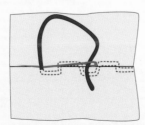

Blind Stitch

Running Stitch

About Debbie Mumm

A talented designer, author, and entrepreneur, Debbie Mumm has been creating charming artwork and quilt designs for more than twenty years.

Debbie got her start in the quilting industry in 1986 with her unique and simple-to-construct quilt patterns. Since that time, she has authored more than fifty book featuring quilting and home decorating projects and has led her business to become a multi-faceted enterprise that includes publishing, fabric design and licensed art divisions.

Known world-wide for the many licensed products that feature her designs, Debbie loves to bring traditional elements together with fresh palettes and modern themes to create the look of today's country.

Designs by Debbie Mumm
Special thanks to my creative teams:

Editorial & Project Design
Carolyn Ogden: Publications & Marketing Manager
Nancy Kirkland: Seamstress/Quilter • Carolyn Lowe: Technical Writer/Editor
Georgie Gerl: Technical Editor • Jackie Saling: Craft Designer
Pam Clarke: Machine Quilter

Book Design & Production
Tom Harlow: Graphics Manager • Heather Butler: Graphic Designer
Kristi Somday: Graphic Designer
Kathy Rickel: Art Studio Assistant • Kris Clifford: Executive Assistant

Photography
Debbie Mumm® Graphics Studio

Art Team
Kathy Arbuckle: Artist/Designer • Heather Butler: Artist

Special Thanks
To John and Pam Greenwood for allowing us to use their
beautiful garden for on-location photography

The Debbie Mumm® Sewing Studio exclusively uses Bernina® sewing machines.

©2007 Debbie Mumm

Discover More from Debbie Mumm®

*Debbie Mumm's®
New Expressions*
96-page, soft cover

*Memories & Milestones
by Debbie Mumm®*
96-page, soft cover

*Seasons
by Debbie Mumm®*
96-page, soft cover

*Just For Fun
by Debbie Mumm®*
112-page, soft cover

Produced by:
Debbie Mumm, Inc.
1116 E. Westview Court
Spokane, WA 99218
(509) 466-3572
Fax (509) 466-6919

www.debbiemumm.com

Published by:
Leisure Arts, Inc
5701 Ranch Drive
Little Rock, AR • 72223
www.leisurearts.com

Available at local quilt shops or at
debbiemumm.com